About the Author

Throughout the course of his youth and adult life George has been focused on the interface between the psychology of Carl Jung and Christian spirituality. This has been expressed first in priestly ministry and spiritual direction, and now in psychotherapy, counselling, peace and nonviolence education and artwork. George is committed to promoting Jung's psychological insights as contemporary spiritual practice for the wellbeing of individuals and for the common good. He lives in Western Australia.

georgetrippe@gmail.com
website: TrippeArt.com

Testimonial statements

On re-reading the manuscript for this book there were quite a few moments when I literally gasped – was it recognition and wonder? Perhaps hints of freedom and hope? It was certainly absolute confidence in the transforming power of inner work in my own life. Walking alongside George as colleague, mentor and friend has deeply influenced how I engage my mind, body and spirit in "the great dialogue" that he so intimately describes. Readers are in for a treat.

Ann Morgan, PhD

As a white practitioner of racial reconciliation in South Africa I find George's embodied, accessible exploration of Nonviolent Spirituality very useful indeed. In our search for deep, sustainable reconciliation I often return in particular to his wise example and clear articulation of shadow work as soul work, individually and collectively.

Wilhelm Verwoerd, PhD

What a gift! George brings clarity and nuance to this soulful exploration of the question, "who am I"? He shares the beautiful insights from his own contemplation of the essence of identity and invites us, through poetic prose, to a journey within. George weaves challenge and compassion, the secular and the sacred, and personal and collective perspectives. The result is an invitation to go ever more deeply on the inner journey, and an inspiration to build a foundation for our sense of self.

Stacie Chappell, PhD

Nonviolent Spirituality:

A Personal Reflection

George E. Trippe, PhD

First published 2022 by George E. Trippe, PhD

Produced by Independent Ink
independentink.com.au

Cover design by Independent Ink
Edited by Stacie Chappell, PhD
Internal design by Independent Ink
Typeset in 12.5/17 pt Adobe Garamond Pro by Post Pre-press Group, Brisbane
Cover image: by the author

ISBN 978-0-6454243-0-0 (paperback)
ISBN 978-0-6454243-1-7 (epub)

Contents

Contents

Introduction

My colleague, Brendan and I sat on the front veranda on a sunny Friday morning. We had agreed to meet together after he spoke to me about his idea. He proposed that we might pool our resources and gifts to create a workshop-retreat experience in peace education around nonviolent living. Brendan brought his long history and lived experience in the socio-political realm, and I brought my psycho-spiritual focus for meaning, and my years of lived experience in the inner way. Our conversations extended over the better part of a year at fortnightly meetings on Friday mornings, usually on my front veranda. Often my wife, Shirley, joined us for a cuppa and then left us to get to work. We arranged and rearranged ideas into a flow of reflections and exercises that slowly took shape under the title of Mainstreaming Nonviolence. We presented this both as a five-day residential experience, and at four weekly gatherings with similar content. This first program design later morphed into an offering that we presented for several years with others, first to young adults and later to people of all ages. What follows here are my reflections that have grown out of my own inner work, out of those initial and many other conversations, and out of the subsequent programs we offered.

There are five chapters to this work. The first, *Locating Myself, Engaging Myself,* starts with me, and with us, as we begin this exercise of reflection. It's about remembering from whence we come, and who and what has influenced us along the way. The second, *Engaging the Mysterious Other,* takes up the experience of the Shadow as put forward in the psychology of Carl G. Jung. This includes the personal and collective Shadow and the golden Shadow. The third chapter, *Reflecting on Essential Matters,* considers issues of relevance to our overall concern for nonviolent living. The fourth chapter looks at *Characteristics of a Nonviolent Spirituality.* The fifth chapter focuses on *Practical Tools to Help Us.* My overall focus for these reflections is to consider how to sustain our commitment to nonviolent living in a world that confronts us with many different and distracting points of view. It is one thing to decide we want to live a nonviolent, peace oriented life, and it is another matter entirely to sustain this commitment day to day. This decision requires ongoing, disciplined reflection in order to maintain this commitment.

I have added the subtitle, "A personal reflection," for this work is just that. Through this work I have become more aware of the limits of my cultures and experiences. My reflections are not complete, and what is here has been edited endlessly. I am aware, like most of us, that my thoughts and ideas are continually changing. Change is the key characteristic of the reflective, creative process for me. Someone once said to me that change is the only experience we can rely on in this life. My life is unfinished and so are many of my thoughts. Life does not stand still.

Over the time of organising these reflections, I have again experienced an insight that indicates this ongoing change. This has to do with language. From my reading, and conversations I have come refer to peace work with three related terms: "non-violence," "peacebuilding" and "cultivating peace." Nonviolence, without the hyphen, is important in affirming this work as an active alternative to violence as a problem solving action. Nonviolence is not a derivative term but refers to the active, intentional work or practice of peace in its own right. It may startle some as an unfamiliar term, and perhaps that is a good thing. I understand that peacebuilding is a common term used internationally to describe the process of peace work. For me it has a quality of being foundational in nature, but can be limited if seen as working from a predetermined blueprint for a process. I have encountered it through the writing of John Paul Lederach in *The Moral Imagination*. I have engaged the metaphor, cultivating peace, through conversations with Wilhelm Verwoerd in South Africa, and his work on the metaphors of peace practice. In terms of practice, this metaphor signals the complexity of the process that requires adaptability, constant attention and a willingness to trust the process as it unfolds. It is a garden metaphor and has the same adventuresome qualities that are experienced and enjoyed by any dedicated gardener.

In 2017 I had the opportunity to visit South Africa and Zimbabwe. I spent the first part of the time with two friends at wildlife reserves, and the other part of my time with my colleague Brendan, engaging people in conversations around nonviolence. On our last day in Johannesburg, we had the privilege to visit the sculpture studio of Pitika Ntali. He was seventy years of age then and known affectionately as *the professor*. The professor, with his staff, was developing a series of very large, black granite sculptures as a history of apartheid. He emphasised that these were not a memorial, but a provocation, an invitation to reflect. The work was very moving, as was his use of the word provocation, and it has stayed with me. In the context of these reflections the word *provocation* represents my hope.

These reflections have grown out of my lived experience, including the ongoing challenges of having to engage and contend with my own capacity for violent responses to life. I find it daily work to sustain the nonviolent way of life to which I aspire. I hope the readers will engage these reflections as an invitation, a provocation to deeper reflection, and a helpful resource in sustaining a nonviolent, peacebuilding way of life.

CHAPTER ONE

Locating Myself, Engaging Myself

Where am I placed?

W e all come from somewhere and bring generations of stories, attitudes, values, traditions, and points of view to our present lives. There are multitudes standing behind each of us. Those from whom I have come have influenced the life I have shaped over the years in both subtle and significant ways. My grandparents on my father's side were Polish immigrants to the United States of America in the early 20th century. My grandfather had been raised in a farming family and continued to be engaged with the land in his new life in the United States. My own parents divorced when I was five and my mother took my brother and me from New York to California to live. I saw my grandfather only two times after that move. From my early childhood I have one image of my grandfather that remains clear. It is of him hoeing among the beans in his garden. Among other things he was a market gardener, and sold his produce door to door. My younger daughter now has the brass-plated scale, certified each year by his city as accurate, that he used in the 1920s to weigh out peoples' purchases.

I come from people who grew food. The foundation wall along the cellar stairs in my grandparents' home was lined with my grandmother's canned produce. All the Polish family grew vegetables. I have done so since I was a boy. I started with radishes because they grow fast. We till the land in our own small ways. It is a part of who we are and how we remain grounded.

My Polish grandparents and family were devout Roman Catholics. I was told more than once that my grandfather walked to mass each morning after he was widowed. It was a memorable morning when I accompanied my aunts and uncle to a mass in Polish in their home church. Though it was not my specific tradition, the experience had a quiet spirit of being home for me.

My mother's family were deeply religious, Protestant people, also of the land in western New York. I am named George for my great grandfather who was a volunteer from New York on the Union side in the Civil War. It interesting for me to note that it is important to me to mention his service in the Civil War. I sometimes have thought that the war is still on. From this side of the family comes the legacy of music and an artistic inclination. My mother's father owned a horse-drawn laundry in New York City and my legacy includes hard working people who prized being self-reliant.

What is the point here? I come from somewhere. We all come from somewhere. Most of us have received stories, heritage, convictions, commitments, and ways of being in the world. Our ancestors contribute more than we sometimes realise. At times my grandfather's spirit feels present with me in my small vegetable garden, and I enjoy this sense of presence. In a sense it feels like I honour both him and me in my modest efforts. I didn't know him well and never learned Polish, yet still we are connected in the garden. My mother's family have gifted me with both a passion for music, a drive to create art, and an enduring attention to things spiritual. Also, I prize my maternal grandfather's entrepreneurial spirit in establishing such a business that was highly successful until his sudden and premature death.

As I concern myself with exploring what for me is a spiritual framework for nonviolent living, my reflections include remembering these ancestors who have bequeathed to me a rich legacy of great variety and grounded energy for living. I am placed in this family, this legacy, these, my people. Here two things seem to be true at the same time: I am my own unique person and have been so all my life, and I come from a people who have given me a heritage of inclinations and interests and a way of being in the world.

At fifteen I was given a set of psychological tests that revealed that I was having trouble coping with the increasing demands of life as a teenager. My parents separated and divorced when I was five. My mother moved us to California to take up new lives. In my growing up years I don't recall meeting another child from a single parent home. I felt the pain of this difference at times very keenly. At age eight I was diagnosed with a heart condition and the reaction around me at the time was to "wrap me in cotton wool." People were protective and I was given every opportunity to avoid responsibilities if I claimed to feel unwell. I learned quickly that this got me out of all sorts of normal expectations as a growing boy.

The result of the testing was that I entered counselling with a man who had studied in Zurich at the Jung Institute and who was also the priest of the local Episcopal Church that had become our home. At this young age of fifteen I was introduced to self-reflection, journal writing and the approach to the soul that is embodied in Carl Jung's psychology. I still chuckle when I remember dashing out of bed and off to an eight o'clock psychology class at the Community College, and then sitting in the back of the room recording my dreams on scraps of paper to place later in my journal. This priest became a giant for me, one who inspired me to life, and was the first of many who guided me and helped me create a soulful framework for living in this world.

Among the giants in my story is Jesus of Nazareth. I risk here sounding simplistic or trite, and yet it is true for me. As a young man growing up in my faith tradition, I felt early on the impact of the Jesus I was coming to know through this tradition and my young spiritual practice. Today, it is more the sense of the Christ archetype expressed through Jesus who continues to inspire, challenge, discomfort and encourage me in the ongoing shaping of my life as shared with others. The Christ/Jesus Tradition is my home base in terms of my spirituality, though I now stand apart from the institutional communities who seek to follow in this way. My focus in recent years is summarised in the phrase, "The Jesus Agenda," and in the question, "How do I put flesh on love?"

I have realised more clearly over the years that this Jesus Tradition is interpreted by me through the lens of Jung's psychological framework. In recent years I have begun to refer to my focus in this work as "psycho-spiritual." I realise that from my youth Jung's approach has been the lens through which I have understood the Jesus story. My first and primary intellectual framework has been Jung's psychology as I experienced it in those early, young years of therapy and reflective practice. Having been introduced to Jung at such an early age and in a context that was both empowering and healing for me, Jung also has been a giant for me. His work continues to influence me in interpreting life, in the attitudes I hold, in reflective practices that give me a sense of well being, and in the actions I take.

These are three among the many who inspire me, my "inspiritors," and the procession of these wonderful people continues today. Some are close to me as friends and colleagues, some have come and gone, and some are known only through their writings, both contemporary and from former times. The influence of these inspiritors places me among countless others who take up a psycho-spiritual path represented by Jesus and Jung, as I seek to sustain my intention to live a nonviolent life. I hope to stand well in this tradition.

Along with my ancestors and inspiritors are the places that have been sacred for me. Countless places have had moments of meaning and among them a few are deeply significant and influential in helping me choose the path that continues to unfold before me. From the age of nine we began attending the local Episcopal Church so that I could sing in the boys' choir. I have fond memories of being in that choir. I still see myself entering the church in procession leading the boys with a friend who shared "first chair" with me. I still hum the parts of the music I sang as my first major solo at age ten and remember much of the duet my friend and I shared. Limited as I was in playing sport because of my heart condition, it was in the choir, and in these experiences, that I had the necessary accomplishments and successes that contributed positively to my self-development.

While the musical experiences were very important to me in my development, the very church property and building became a place of safety and grounding for me. I remember often walking onto the property and entering the worship space and feeling some sense of being grounded and safe. It was almost like being home. The last time I visited there, the property and the worship space still held a deep sense of home for me. The experiences of my youth in that place have been very significant in shaping me. These include singing in the choirs, listening to sermons, meeting with friends for conversation in the youth groups, attending dinners, and sitting in the nave at night alone or with a friend praying for whatever the issues were at the time. Home, it had a sense of home. From time to time the town and the church appear in dreams to remind me of these creative experiences in my youth.

I was fifteen or sixteen when I was invited to attend a men's retreat at Mt. Calvary Retreat House above Santa Barbara in California. It was the West coast Monastery of the Episcopal Church's Order of Holy Cross. From that year on, I visited there with some regularity to make retreats or just to rest between semesters at the university. My wife Shirley and I actually made a retreat there one year as part of our wedding anniversary! This, too, became a spiritual home and in my late teens I had given consideration to exploring the possibility of joining the Order. Some years later I did become an Associate of the Community and still remember the sense of deep belonging and home that I felt in that connection. It was for years a place where so many deeply important moments occurred.

The monastery sat on a rise in the lower hills of the mountains, and with little effort I could hike up into a canyon along a stream for times of exercise, quiet reflection and writing. Quite a distance up the canyon there is a rock, large and quite flat, to which I returned many times to have that quiet time. It remains vivid in my memory as a sacred site though I left that part of the world now more than thirty years ago. The last time I visited the monastery before migrating to Australia, I wept as I drove down the hill and began my drive home. No other place in my historical landscape has ever evoked those tears. The monastery is now gone, having been caught up in a hills fire above Santa Barbara in recent years. For me, it remains a sacred place now in memory.

On my historical landscape there are the gardens. I can remember as far back as age ten growing those radishes and some portulacas along the side yard next to the garage. My garden has been a moveable sacred place wherever I have lived. These various gardens have helped place me on the land and grounded me in a life that precedes me and will continue on after my time here. There have been the vegetables but flowers as well. I am deeply moved by the riots of colour that flowers produce. Something in me feels very connected to their stunning presentation. The vegetables do more than feed my body. Even now I continue to find simple calm and solace sitting on a limestone column among my vegetables and simply contemplating their lives. And, yes, I do talk to my vegies and greet the flowering portulacas on the verandah edge.

I suppose, on reflection, this relationship with sacred places extends widely to landscapes and nature in general. In my last two years of university, I attended the University of Southern California in Los Angeles (USC). There on campus I discovered a tree that in spring had new leaves that were of the most beautiful yellow green. I often went at midday and sat on a bench across from the tree and contemplated its beauty. The radiant colour gave me a wonderful sense of peace. In the evenings of spring, I sometimes walked with a friend in the rose garden at the nearby stadium enjoying our conversation and the riot of colours and fragrances of the wonderful display.

When life invited me into a depression in my early thirties, I learned to walk along the ocean shoreline just where the water lapped onto the sand. It is a liminal space, a place of intersection that, for me, became a place of calm. Many hours have been spent in such walking, or just sitting reading and resting near the ocean. The timeless rhythms of waves lapping or crashing on the shore speak deeply to me. Places such as these, and many others in moments here and there, became sacred and not only grounded me in my own life but also stirred in me a deep sense of being part of something larger than myself. I have sacred places, sacred sites, in my history that have been of significance for both my spirit and soul, and that have thereby contributed to my desire and capacity to choose and sustain a nonviolent way of life.

My ancestors, inspiritors, and sacred places all assist me in locating myself in my own life and in the larger life I share with all others. These also encourage this desire to reflect on a spirituality that will support nonviolent living and contribute to peace. I realise that I stand grounded on values and principles that are a part of this spiritual framework. At this point I wish to remember only one story that has shaped me more than I realised at the time. When I was twenty-one, I was called up to take a physical examination to determine my eligibility for being drafted into military service in the United States. At the time, Shirley and I were engaged to be married, and our wedding date was less than two months away. I passed the military physical, but then was classified toward the bottom of the list of eligible persons as I also had been accepted by my church denomination as a theological student. This status resulted in an exemption from service. The outcome of this process was the realisation that I had no heart for military involvement in any way. I could find no place in myself to submit to the expectations of military life. It had no place in the landscape of my life. I won't pretend to have thought this through carefully at the time; getting married took precedence. What I did know was that I did not trust military solutions to differences. At that time and over the years, I was not required to make a public declaration in this matter, and yet I knew that my own path was more given to cultivating peace in whatever ways I could. Largely this passion has been expressed in focusing on soul work in the one to one model that I have crafted through the influences of the Christ/Jesus Tradition and Jung's psycho-spiritual work. In recent years this has become more conscious and intentional, as I have worked with colleagues to share in facilitating gatherings focussed on nonviolent interfaith leadership. This brush with the military was my first real experience of understanding that I did not support the dominant culture in which I was living. I was, in this instance, counter-cultural.

Community

The ancestors, inspiritors, and the places all form an initial framework for exploring nonviolent spirituality. The intention in these initial reflections is to locate me in my own landscape and in the larger life landscape as well. Woven into this tapestry of these influences that tell me from whence I come is the deep and substantial influence of culture. I come from a specific cultural time and place that helps shape my character, values and sense of how to be in this world. Much of this has been filtered through family, education, faith traditions, and through inspiritors as well. I was born and grew up in mid twentieth century America. Though born in the greater New York City area, my growing up years were in the greater eastern suburbs of Los Angeles. The years of our growing up were safe and simple. I predate television; we played outside a lot all over the neighbourhood and walked with others to and from school. Our world was very local as kids, I have no standout memories of larger world events in my childhood. It was in my early teens that things changed. Sputnik was up there, bomb threats were down here and taken seriously as we practiced "drop" drills in classes in junior high. "Drop" was one word you dare not yell out loud in school in those days. Also at junior high we were integrated with the black students from the "other" part of town. We had real estate segregation; it was never discussed. This was not the first time for me to engage black people. During my semester at home with the heart condition, my main day carer was a young black woman, Elaine, who was my only real friend during those months and I still hold her in fond memory. Even with this experience, I now see that my discomfort with difference, especially with black people, was well entrenched through the unspoken attitudes and values of my various community cultures, including family and faith. We integrated teens attended school and community dances, but we did not really engage much beyond these, and when we did it was awkward and there were separate groups in the spaces. Only once do I remember entering the home of black family, and no black child ever entered mine. Our church congregation was only white as I remember, except for the black woman, Dora, who was the soloist in the soprano section of the choir.

We all come from somewhere, and this is a very brief sketch of the very white culture of my early years that has had a deep influence on me, and remnants of which remain in my history and psyche. All these influences make their contribution in a greater or lesser degree, to my sense of community. Over decades I have been more, and less at times, conscious of moving into new understandings of culture – more complex, multi-cultural, a rainbow of people as Desmond Tutu describes South Africa today. I need to remember from whence I come. These people, these sacred places, this cultural history, continue with me, and now and then have their influence in my daily living as I seek to contribute to peace work and nonviolent living.

Before we shift focus in this area of community, and we will come back to it later on, I want to bring in one relatively new and important sense of community. I acknowledge that in recent years I have come to value as essential honouring the fact that I am part of the one community, that is inclusive of all creation here on planet earth. This is the global human and creation community – all life on our island home. In recent years I became aware of the photos taken by the Voyager I spacecraft of the planet earth from the edge of our galaxy, and of the reflection by Carl Sagan on the pale blue dot. As we do these days, I googled the pale blue dot photos and was struck with awe by the tiny dot that is our home in that large cosmic scape. It moves me deeply to see "us" from this perspective. I keep a part of the "pale blue dot" statement that Sagan made years ago as part of my personal devotional readings.

I have placed one of the NASA photographs of planet earth in my entry hallway as a reminder of this larger community to which I belong and on which I depend. My fantasies include creating a greeting card or poster using a photo of planet earth with the words. "Love it, 'cause you can't leave it." It's my update on the "Love it or leave it," statement that was used some years ago to shut down conversation and efforts toward creating new and inclusive visions for life together. Planet earth, the only home we have; presently there is nowhere else to go.

My outer communities have included my original and adopted nations, my state, for many years the church, the local neighbourhood, my personal and valued friends, and my family community. These also serve to locate me in my own life landscape and in the larger life landscape we share. These communities also answer my soul's need both to belong and to feel safe in the living of my days. Having reflected on my sense of location in the wider landscape, and touched briefly on the communities that are the context of this belonging, I want now to consider the experience of community in a different way as I continue to reflect on a spirituality that will support nonviolent living and make way for peace.

Community within

I have thus far reflected on ways that help me locate myself in my outer life. Ancestors, inspiritors, and places all help me locate myself not only in my life, but also in the larger life that we all share. I want now to use the image of community turned inward, as a way of engaging the rich, complex and sometimes quite mysterious event that I encounter as "myself." My ongoing question is, "How can we employ the community image to help us engage ourselves more deeply as we seek a nonviolent, spiritual framework?"

It has been forty years ago now that I came upon the notion of the inner village as a way to honor and contain the complexity of my soul. This part of my journey began with a dream that came to me while I was engaged in a Jungian analysis with a rather quiet and clever man named Weyler Greene. In the dream I see a beautiful Garden of Eden like scene. The garden is a very serene place and a sense of completeness emanates from it. In the middle of this garden there are two animals, gazelle like, which are about to couple. Suddenly in from the left storms a huge grizzly bear hell-bent on causing utter destruction. As he tears into things I did the only sensible thing to do; I woke up! I was very shaken. I took this dream to my next appointment with Weyler and after listening to the story he suggested that I talk to the grizzly bear. I had been at this process of soul work long enough to take him seriously, and so in the next week I re-entered the dream story.

I imagined the scene, the beautiful garden, the vibrant animals about to couple, and then in storms the bear. As he is about to tear into things, I enter the scene and yell, "Stop! What are you doing? Who are you?" The grizzly bear looks down on me – remember that when standing these bears are very tall – and says, "I am your anger." Another whole dimension of my journey began at that moment. This was the first experience I had with what Jung termed active imagination.

While I did not return to have further conversations with the bear, I was now open to the notion that "others" were a part of who I am. Not long after this event I had a dream featuring a Great Dane dog that became the occasion through which an inner community, or village, began to take shape. The Great Dane, named "Dog," took me into deep places where I discovered significant others who became the early inhabitants of the village.

Through the years I have found others who speak of the inner community in similar ways. James Hillman, the Jungian Analyst, speaks of the boardinghouse where everyone is included, even the rather odd ones. Thomas Moore, a theologian and counselor, speaks of the soulful community where sometimes someone other than our usual self seems to be in control. We know this most commonly through the experiences of artistic people who speak of the muse who guides and directs the creative process. John O'Donohue, a theologian in the Celtic tradition, writes of the crowd within the individual heart. He writes that this crowd is so numberless that we can never act out in our lives all the aspects of our inner selves.

So, there is a community within me. I am a village, a family. How does this community take shape? The inner community forms up quite naturally over time. Very often a character will emerge in a dream, who has intense and mysterious significance for me and who then becomes a part of my inner family. A recent newcomer to the village is one named "Resistant," who does not like at all the disciplines associated with writing! In other instances I have become aware of a behavior or attitude in me that is very influential in my conscious living. I find it is easier to understand this one if I give it a sense of being a personality, what Hillman calls a sub-personality. This helps me to be more conscious of its influence in my daily life. What in other models of personality may be referred to as characteristics, here I give the sense of being a person, part of the complex personal village family.

Examples of the characters who will emerge in the village are many, and it is important to understand that the cast of characters will be different for each of us. There are thematic types that take individual expression in our own interior experiences. For many there is the old wise man or the old wise crone, and often the child, or children, will appear in various forms and at various ages, depending on the personal history of the individual. Some people encounter a high achiever who is ambitious for success at any cost, others realise there is a very conservative one or radically progressive one, or both, in the village. Often a needy one will emerge, as might the anxious one, and the frightened one. For some the adventurer is an important village figure, for others it may well be the artist, the poet, or the dramatic one. Some find the socially correct one to have a strong voice in the village, for others it is the anti-social one or the wild one.

It is not unusual for people to find a religious or spiritual figure in the inner community. It could be a female or male shaman, a Merlin-like magician, a mystic, a Mary or Christ figure. Each of these will vary according to the needs of the individual whose village it is. One young man raised in a very conservative Christian religious framework encountered a Christ figure who arrived dressed in a loincloth, carrying his own cross and exhibiting a great familiarity with foul language. This Christ figure was a compensatory image to the overly polite and pious tradition in which this person had lived and by which he felt burdened. He needed a very different image of a savior to facilitate the discernment necessary for the maturation of his identity, as both distinct from, and part of, these influences.

Another man, burdened by an overly serious interpretation of his Christian faith tradition, encountered a God, or Abba, figure of great hilarity, who caused the villagers often to laugh with great glee at his straw hat and cane antics on a jet ski. Again, this man also needed a very different God figure to compensate for the burden under which he had been living. It is important to acknowledge and understand that these religious figures are psychological aspects of the individual's psyche and come in these various forms according to individual need. How we connect these images to the central, and/or divine, figures, revered by faith traditions, is a secondary consideration. I have concluded for myself that there is a connection between the images of the faith tradition and the psychological images of the individual at some deep level that may well challenge the conventional or dominant ways in which these religious figures are perceived.

There can be healers, compassionate ones; there can also be selfish, greedy ones, one who represents our capacity for violence, and yet another who is our peacemaker. There can be animals in the village as well. The Great Dane, Dog, has been with me now for these forty years, and is now a quiet presence in the village. The list goes on and on and is unique to each of us.

As noted above, this notion of the inner community, the village is a profound and simple exercise of giving personal images to what others might see as characteristics of personality. It is a conscious and intentional exercise, and is a tool that can lead to a greater, richer sense of self, and to a broader understanding of the complexity of who we are. It also gives us a way of relating more personally with the many aspects, or persons, who make up our personality, our character.

How might we describe the importance and function of the village model of personality? Simply put, it is a model of personality that assists us in forging a welcoming, accepting, and friendly home for all of the complex parts of who we are. It gives us a way to acknowledge our many aspects of personality, and to work for peace and harmony within ourselves. It is my conviction that without this effort, without making peace within, without interacting with the diverse villagers as to how to live, we cannot sustain a mature, nonviolent spiritual framework, either in attitude or practice. If we can't make peace with ourselves, if we can't be nonviolent with ourselves, we will struggle to offer these qualities to others. For me, it begins with me.

We can identify several distinct benefits to undertaking the village model of our personalities. First, we are able to honour the soul's complexity, our ambivalences, contradictions and paradoxes. With this we are able to abandon the notion that life is simple and that we are to strive for a simple sense of self. Simplicity is a great virtue. My lived experience now teaches me that simplicity emerges slowly over time out of our ongoing, creative dialogue with our natural diversity and complexity. It is like drops of gold dripping from the swirling cauldron of our lives.

To seek simplicity without embracing our complexity is to risk falling into premature certainties that trap us in either/or thinking and that fuel an adversarial relationship to ourselves and then to others. Odd as it may seem, the soul work with the inner village has allowed me to grow toward a way of life in which the core principles and values for my life are being distilled from this complex soul that I still claim as mine.

Second, the inner community or village model assists me in establishing a working relationship with myself. The work is simply to make enemies friends, and to make room for all in the village. No one is excluded; all belong. For me, the catch phrase that challenges me is "radical inclusivity." I have here a model that allows me to work for peace among the different parts of me, and to welcome, accept and come to love, those who I previously denied and refused to acknowledge. This, at times, can be very difficult. There are times when I stand in awe of the diverse persons who are parts of me and can only shake my head.

It is important to note that to give space to all in the village is not the same as giving all villagers access to outside reality. Some of my villagers remain in the village. As I like to say, not everyone gets to go out to play.

Third, the model of the inner village allows me to come to such a peace with my own diversity and complexity that I am able to offer a space of hospitality and safety to others who can then risk growing into a deeper, more peaceful sense of themselves through this intriguing way of seeing ourselves. Peace with myself makes it possible for me to enable the peace of others.

Part of Me

Somewhere along the way I came upon a language tool that has been very helpful to me in working from this inner village model. It is simply, "Part of me." It is very simple and very liberating. It helps us honor our complexity within and takes the pressure off of us having to be single minded, decisive, clear and in control at all times. In my lived experience, these qualities are fleeting at best. I am learning that at times maturity includes confusion, chaos, and internal conflict. Maturity includes not knowing, great ambivalence, contradiction, paradox and mystery. In spite of all this valuable and important soul work, sometimes I baffle me.

This language tool is often expressed as "part of me this, and part of me that." Part of me is progressive and forward-looking and part of me is very conservative. Part of me is generous and part of me is selfish and stingy with what is mine. Part of me wants deeply to help others and part of me is in it for myself. This complexity goes on and on and has led me to accept the truth that, for me, there is rarely a simple, pure motive. Often we are divided in the face of significant needs and decisions. The "part of me" language tool enables us to remain more honest with ourselves as we navigate this life and intend to live within the framework of a nonviolent spirituality.

We are complex. The inner community image opens us up to a broad and rich spectrum of our selves. We find people who surprise us, disquiet our conventional sense of self, and people who contradict each other with differing points of view. Engaging ourselves as an inner village or community, allows us finally to come to peace with our own complexity and to navigate more consciously and intentionally the nonviolent way of living that we desire.

The Great Dialogue

The way in which we are able to engage our inner community is the simple practice of dialogue. Dialogue enables us to interact with our villagers in ongoing conversations and negotiations over the living of our lives, and makes it possible to acknowledge and contain our diverse inner community in lively and peaceful ways.

A major result of this dialogic practice is that we realise that we have many interior resources for making our decisions and creating the necessary strategies for living day to day. Our limited conscious minds have lots of help in determining directions to take, responses to offer, insights to consider, and various opinions on which to reflect. The dialogic process can offer us a great sense of relief as we realise that we have inner resources in the form of diverse villagers who can help us sort and sift through the many challenges and responsibilities of living.

This dialogic process is referred to as active imagination in Jung's psychological framework. It is an inner dialogue, wherein the conscious personality engages the relevant people or animals in the village. The dialogue experience is framed as a dialogue between equals, and is characterized by respectful listening and mutual interaction even if at times it becomes intense and passionate. The goal is to gain a broader perspective on matters at hand than our conscious minds can attain alone. The dialogue allows for, insists on, uncensored interactions wherein parts of us, the inner villagers, are able to contribute their diverse points of view on any given issue. We can often be surprised at the wisdom that is hidden in the depths of our own souls that will emerge when we allow these others to speak their opinions. The process allows us to honor the sometimes complex and complicated responses we have to situations at hand, and in such reflections to make decisions that serve us well and may also be beneficial to others. All this has the capacity to assist us in living more nonviolently.

James Hollis, in his writing, refers to this dialogue as lifelong, ongoing and continuous. It is a tool, a method a practice that enables us to develop a broader self-understanding. In this more comprehensive self-knowing, I affirm that we attain a new level of personal wholeness through the acceptance of our complexity. We are able also to develop a deeper sense of confidence in our personal authority in our own lives through a great reliance our own inner wisdom.

While this process of inner dialogue may help us in imme-diate circumstances to address specific and daily issues, more importantly it becomes a preferred way to engage life as a whole. What we begin to value as an enriching interior process can quite naturally extend to become the customary way in which we encounter others and all of life. This dialogue process has the potential to help us be more sensitive to the complexities of others and to their very diverse approaches to life. We are able to engage differences with more ease. Our openness in dialogue assists us in engaging others more freely in collaborative learn-ing and in sharing the inner wisdom that we each carry in the depths of our souls.

Part of the pleasure of my involvement with nonviolence and peacebuilding has been the recovery of the experience of conversation. With colleagues we often talk of opening a conver-sation with others to explore a possibility, an issue or a potential project. I see now that in past interactions too much of my energy has been posturing to support a point of view in order to persuade others to my way of being in the world. Part of this has been influenced by my training and was a way to carry a certain authority in my professional work, and part has been my need for power and control to feel safe in this complex world. Respectful, reflective and open conversation is essential not only to the dialogue we have within, but also in the conversations we share with others. Dialogic conversation allows us to engage differing points of view with interest and care. This conversation has the potential to cultivate a healthy, nonviolent sense of community with others.

Recently I have found that I am beginning to consider the image of dialogue as the preferred and overriding image of our interactions on wider levels as well. I am now inclined to see life as The Great Dialogue. It is interesting to consider how I see myself in dialogue with my larger communities and my nation, indeed with the human family. This form of dialogue moves beyond the exchange of words to a sense of interaction in receiving information through awareness and forming a response to it. What is being "said" to me in how others live by choice or by the oppression of others? How can I live in ways that "speak" to them of our connectedness and of their value and dignity?

I have begun in recent times to extend this Great Dialogue as an image that has great value for me in relating to nature, to the creation, and to all life on our planet with whom we share life. What is the nonverbal dialogue, the ongoing conversation, with my garden, the local parklands, forests, plains, deserts, household pets, food animals, animals in the wild, waterways, water bodies, the air we breathe? What have we to "say" to each other? Nonverbal dialogic interaction for me underscores the efforts of environmental conservation, sustainability and health. How do we speak without words to each other, live together and support each other on this planet earth, our shared home?

As I mentioned earlier, many years ago I was invited into a time of depression. It came on suddenly and I was fortunate to have helpful counsel close to me in order to engage this strange visitor in meaningful ways. During this time I lived with varying states of anxiety. In speaking of sacred places, I mentioned a place that became important for me, a place where I felt calm and safe. This was walking along the shoreline at a nearby beach. I can still recall that sense of calm in walking slowly along in the shallow waters that washed up on the sand. In that place and in those moments I felt that I was going to be okay. The action of the waters on the sands, the interaction of the two seem to be telling me that I was part of a larger picture that had meaning and purpose far beyond what my fragile consciousness could at that time under-stand. That liminal space where water and sand danced a timeless dance spoke deeply to me and grounded me in something deeper than my present fragile state. I still can recall and recover that sense of being grounded with a walk along the shoreline.

Some years ago I was making a retreat at a monastery in country Australia when a fierce storm went quickly through the area. I spent the entire afternoon until dark assisting the one brother of the Community who was at home clearing brush and debris, and a fallen tree over the driveway. The next morning I began clearing pathways and at one point became frustrated. I had come on retreat to do some reading and deep reflection on a project of importance to me, and here I was sweeping and clearing walkways! In that moment a voice within me said, "Read the trees!" This encouraged me to be mindful of where I was and attentive to what surrounded me. What I became aware of was the wonderful diversity of shapes, colors, sizes, ages and stages of growth. The trees and shrubs "spoke" to me of diversity, which is an essential sign of health not only to the bush, but also to the human community and to my soul. It was a renewing experience.

Middle Night Visitations

For more years than I can now remember, I have often wakened in the night anywhere between two and four. Usually I come awake from a dream, other times it is that I need to use the toilet. More often than not, my mind kicks in quickly and I lay in bed for a while as thoughts wander here and there. Sometimes I will get up and make a list of what is rumbling around and then return to sleep. Many times I have lain awake and annoyed, thrashing around until sleep wins the moment. A conversation with a friend some time ago has brought me to a different place. We were talking about these visitations, and he told me he makes no room for the harsh or critical thoughts that would come, but dismisses them and gets up to make a cup of tea. I realized in this conversation that this was not an option for me. It became clear that these thoughts, especially the negative ones, were imbued with a meaning and purpose of their own and I needed to attend upon them in some way. They had claimed this time and space and needed to be heard. It is a form of dialogue, part of The Great Dialogue.

I have come to refer to this experience as the "middle night visitation," and have learned to let them play out without too much interference. These middle night reflections run the gamut from violent, vengeful scenarios wherein, in my mind, the unjust get their just desserts, to pondering alternative ways I could have acted in situations that have left me discomforted. Middle night often gives room to the most violent voices in my village. At other times I work on a collage or painting in my mind trying new techniques, juxtaposing materials and shapes and sometimes sketching leaves and small branches. In less frequent moments I imagine singing for others songs that are meaningful to my history with a voice full and rich with tone and breadth. Now and then, in the dark of the night, I compose parts of the ideas and stories that later become written reflections. In fact, this very reflection on the middle night visitations, took its original shape in middle night. In these moments the golden energy of creativity emerges and expresses itself variously in flowing emotions, rhapsodic melody, and harsh and difficult expressions of indignation.

Middle night reflections sometimes shock me with the intensity of their violence, and I realise this energy for such violence is within me and needs to be acknowledged. At other times middle night expressions move me deeply and I find a strong desire in me to bring something of their extraordinary beauty into material form in my waking life. These times remind me that there is a deep well of creativity in my soul reaching down into and fed by what I name as the divine life, and intimations of it often do make it to the page or paper in my daytime efforts at the creative expression.

Middle night is increasingly important to me, as I have realized that it is a time when the censoring, defensive functions of the ego are less active, and intense, raw images will often come through from the unconscious. Whatever these experiences may be, they are part of the wholeness of who I am, and they need to be acknowledged and honored if I am going to sustain a nonviolent way of life. In the middle night, the unconscious speaks, and dialogue continues. If I push the negative thoughts away, dismiss them and deliberately distract myself, I dishonor parts of myself. In this action, I refuse the dialogue and set myself up for other, more problematic, visitations, perhaps at times when I will regret their appearing. If I push away the golden moments of the night, again I refuse the dialogue, and I may lose access to the very sacred creativity that I otherwise long to have inspire my creative work. Middle night has become, for me, an important part of The Great Dialogue, and contributes to my sense of completeness and my capacity to move into nonviolent living.

Life is The Great Dialogue. It seems to me that nonviolent living and spiritual practice are greatly supported and sustained by an attitude of many dialogues in life. If dialogue can become our usual way of being, then we are more able to listen openly to the diverse, intimidating and colorful villagers, to the diverse others who interact with our lives, to the many diverse communities in which we share, to the diverse others with whom we do not agree, and to the larger creation of which we are a part and on which we depend for our very lives.

In these initial reflections my focus has been on locating myself in my own life, and acknowledging the various communities in which I share. I have also turned the image of community inward to consider the diverse aspects of my own soul that are all parts of me. Finally I have reflected on life as dialogue, and the ongoing conversations with the wondrous diversity of myself, with others and the creation. All these considerations help to inform us as we explore a spirituality that supports and sustains nonviolent living and the making of peace.

CHAPTER TWO

Engaging the Mysterious Other

In the first chapter of these reflections on a spiritual framework that will sustain nonviolent living, we have touched briefly on our sense of place and heritage, the experience of community both outer and inner, and the dynamic of dialogue as a way to characterise living with ourselves, with others, and with all of humanity and creation. In this second chapter I intend to explore the concept and experience of the shadow as identified and defined by Carl Jung in his psychological work, and extended in the subsequent endeavours of many who work with Jung's psychological framework.

From my point of view, the shadow is one of Jung's most important contributions to our self-understanding of the Other within, and to this Other in our various relationships and communities. I intend to reflect on the shadow as a personal experience in both our internal landscape and in our relationships. Also, I will focus on the collective nature of the shadow and its place in our wider relationships and interactions, from friends to nations. We will explore both the negative and positive and aspects of our shadow experiences.

What is this shadow?

From my reading of Jung and those who follow in his work, I conclude that the notion of the opposites was key to his under-standing of the psyche. As I see it, Jung took his lead from nature, since he saw the psyche as part of nature. In nature we have exam-ples of opposites relating in complementary ways. Night leads into day and day into night. We experience male and female, hot and cold, liquid and solid, left and right, living and dead, up and down, straight and winding. Each part of these pairs in their var-iations informs the other. Susan Cain, in her book, *Quiet*, about introversion, uses the phrase "complementary pairings." It seems a bit less adversarial, and emphasises strongly the notion that the pairs belong together in some way.

The persona and the shadow are complementary opposites; it is the pairing with which we are concerned here. The persona is that part of our personality that functions to relate us to the world around us. It is the carefully constructed mask we place over the ego in our interactions with others. The persona is the socialised us and is to some degree conscious and intentional as we choose how to navigate our way in our various relationships and circumstances. It is a mask we choose that both reveals us in measured degrees and conceals much of who we are. Classic experiences of the persona include the "me" present when at a job interview, on a first date, and at a social gathering. It is my persona who engages sales persons in various stores or markets, the lifeguards at my swimming pool, waitpersons in a restaurant, and a group of people to whom I am making a presentation. The persona is shaped both by cultural influences and my inner need to be connected successfully to others. It is characterised often by good manners, polite and witty conversation, interested listening, and all around affable behaviours that win family and friends to me. I often tell myself that the persona is me diluted down to a tolerable degree!

The shadow is the mysterious Other within. The shadow is the reverse side of the persona that carries the opposite traits of the personality, the other part of the pair. It contains everything that has been repressed and rejected by us because these traits do not fit in with the ego ideal that we have cultivated from our early years. Family, faith tradition and social cultures greatly influence this process of forming the shadow and we are motivated in this by our desire to be accepted, to belong and to be loved.

For this reason our initial understanding of the shadow is that it is negative in content. In dream work the shadow is usually the first "other" we encounter as it is most often close to the surface. In dream imagery the shadow usually appears in the same gender as the dreamer, though in some circumstances the shadow is provoked by the irritating behaviour of the opposite gender. The shadow is everything we consciously are not. She, or he, is the one we do not desire to be, and we have been told it is not good to be, and therefore, the one we can't imagine ourselves to be. This shadow content then is the undesirable us, and is often somewhat underdeveloped, inferior and crude in expression, because we have little practice in expressing this part of us. This shadow Other contains all those less attractive, impractical, uncivilised, rude and even animal-like emotions and attitudes. These are clearly incompatible with our conscious, conventional personality that we have both chosen and taken on to make our way in the world.

This shadow Other wants to do those things we could never allow ourselves to do, and those things we would not dream of doing when in our "right," that is, conscious minds. The shadow harbours all those attitudes and desires of which we are ashamed, even if we are only slightly conscious of them. Here is all we do not want to know of us, all that we don't want to admit to or own up to. The shadow, is the mysterious and troublesome Other within.

What by nature are complementary opposites or pairings, easily become conflicted opposites in our choosing one trait over another by choice and cultural influences. This is the terrain of the inner life that often feels like a civil war.

The shadow is part of the personal unconscious that develops as we grow up and are encouraged to choose certain desirable characteristics and traits. The shadow also has a collective dimension as we share attitudes with others that are commonly held in our cultures. These include negative attitudes toward people who are different in a variety of ways. Difference is often a trigger point for activating negative Shadow for both individuals and groups. However, this collective dimension has a yet deeper and more dangerous aspect in light of the energies of the collective unconscious that can rise up in a community standing for their conscious way of being in the world and demonising others who represent the denied opposite, the shadow of the group. Racial discrimination is a classic example. The shadow is not only the mysterious and troublesome Other within us; it also can be manifest as a collective shadow in our shared lives with others when we express a negative attitude toward groups of others who are different.

The personal experience of shadow

The shadow grows in our personal inner lives as we learn to disown parts of who we are through repression. What we disown sinks into the unconscious and stands in opposition to the ideal we have both been given and have adopted for our own.

There are some quick exercises we can undertake to get a sense of our personal shadow. First, we can make a list of the virtues we were given and have taken on as noble and good, and next to each write its opposite. For instance, most of us can remember easily those parental one-liners that we received in various circumstances that helped shape our way of living. Here we have insight into shadow. We can expand this further by remembering as well family teachings that define a virtue. The opposite characteristic will reveal our shadow. Examples include: "Honesty is the best policy;" "it is always best to tell the truth;" "don't hit your brother/sister;" and "it is not nice to be angry." The personal shadow will then contain the opposite of the virtues and preferred behaviours. In my growing up years in a single parent home, hard work was valued and expected, so being lazy was a shadow trait that often troubled me. Out of this tension I came into my adult years, and my marriage, with no real understanding of leisure. It was my wife who helped me learn how to relax.

Another way to engage shadow is to pay attention to those others who annoy or upset us in any way. Whenever I am uncomfortable and compulsively reviewing some event, another person's action or opinion, I can be sure that shadow is close at hand. Years ago I read Jung's memoir, *Memories, Dreams, Reflections*. I memorised a simple statement from the chapter on "Travels," that stuck with me and that invites me to attend to the personal shadow. Jung states "Everything that irritates us about others can lead us to an understanding of ourselves."

What these examples teach us is that we usually meet shadow first in our negative projections onto others. Unconscious, negative projections that are not examined seriously inhibit our capacities to sustain a spiritual practice that is nonviolent and that builds peace. The unacknowledged negative projection is a major source of violence on every level of community in our daily living. This includes the violence toward ourselves in our inner villages and to the global human family. The rule of thumb is simply that if we will not engage our shadow projections when we encounter them, we will continue to project negatively onto others and support some form of violence toward those others. To say it another way, we can easily identify a person's shadow by the enemies she or he keeps.

While the shadow is often seen as negative, it is not, therefore, evil. It is a way in which evil impulses and systems can gain our attention and our allegiance, and yet in itself it is simply the other side of our conscious ego ideal. To engage this consciously, and intentionally, diminishes greatly the possibility that we will support attitudes and actions, personal and collective, which have the potential to manifest evil. It is important to stress here that to engage the shadow does not mean that we act it out. To engage the shadow is an important aspect of our inner work and the engagement is often through disciplined reflection, journal writing, or talking issues through with a trusted companion. It is to contain the energy in what we now see as our inner village.

Examples of our personal shadow abound in our everyday living. Here are some examples from my own experience. In the last town I lived in while in California, I was standing on the sidewalk in front of the house waiting for my wife, Shirley, to come out to the car so that we could go do our errands. As I stood there, a teenage boy ran down the street on the sidewalk across from me. As I watched him run, I wondered what might be wrong. Then, in a moment of reflection, I wondered why anything had to be wrong. He was a teenager running. Maybe he was late to catch a bus, or dashing to the shops nearby, or running because it was simply fun to run. Why was anything wrong? I realised in that moment that I assumed something was wrong because he was a Latino teenager. I reckon that if he had been the blond teenager at the top of the street I would have had an entirely different reaction. In that moment I was confronted with the subtle shadow of the racism that was part of growing up white in that culture. I have long concluded that the collective racism of the American psyche infects and contaminates all who live or have lived in that culture for any length of time. I would suggest that this kind of collective shadow attitude can be true in any culture. We take on the shadow of the culture by virtue of our living in it. In my experience, it is as if the racist point of view was in the air we breathed. Countless experiences of my own, experiences shared in conversations, and reports in the media have contributed to this shadow content. Part of me is racist. He lives in the village. It is humiliating to acknowledge this, but it is essential to be honest with myself so that I might choose consciously to build peace and live a nonviolent way of life.

One evening I had visited a friend who lived at a university residential college in Perth. To return home I decided to drive along the river and through the centre of the city. At night, with all the lights reflecting on the water it is a lovely drive. When I arrived at a stoplight in the city centre, I noticed people on the street and locked my car door. What? I almost never lock my car doors, in spite of my nagging and concerned family! Why did I do this on this night? Why at that intersection? I realised that I was projecting my shadow fear of the unknown onto that scene, the strangers, and the darkness of the city night.

Once, while reading an interesting novel, I found one character a little disturbing and over a few days just didn't seem to find the time to get back to reading the novel. Finally I questioned myself as to what was going on, and I realised that this particular character was a very clear picture of my shadow at my worst. The character was selfish in the extreme, and insensitive to the needs of others. The phrase we toss around in jest is "It's all about me." Well it was all about the character in the novel, and there are times when it's all about me as well. I sometimes secretly mumble that if everyone around me would do as I ask, require or demand, we'd all be happier! Maybe you know this person as well. Once I processed this I was able to finish the novel. By the way the character didn't fare too well in the end!

Finally, years ago I read an article in the local newspaper wherein a public figure I knew somewhat made a disparaging remark about another public figure. I was annoyed for several days as I thought the first man was projecting wildly his shadow onto the second. After a few days I realised I was projecting my shadow onto the first man who was projecting onto the second! It was all about power. If I confess that my peers in senior high school at one time called me "Bonaparte," when I was chairing a teenage committee to plan social events for teens in the city, perhaps that trail of projections makes some sense! Ah, the shadow!

Others too have shared shadow stories over the years. A young man who struggled with his self-confidence, told of disappointing his father as a boy while fishing, and was crossly told, "You'll never amount to anything!" A young woman who was beginning to engage dating young men told of being called a slut as a teenager because she came in shortly after her curfew. Whose shadows are operative here? Another young man told of his shock when walking down the aisle to receive communion at mass, he found himself internally rehearsing his vocabulary of foul language. Yet another woman who worked in the beauty industry was really unnerved when an old dirty, messy woman appeared in her quiet reflection one day and who seemed to want to talk with her.

This personal shadow is a part of our nature and our every-day experience. Images like these come to us daily. This is not a problem to be fixed. We don't get rid of our shadow. Our challenge here is to acknowledge our personal shadow experiences and to learn how to deal with them consciously over a lifetime. As Jung says, "Everything that irritates us about others, can lead us to an understanding of ourselves." We will return to this task later on.

The Collective Shadow

I am indebted to James Hollis in his book, *Why Good People Do Bad Things*, for provoking and clarifying many ideas in this section. The other dimension of the shadow we live with, and that influences our spiritual attitudes and practices, is the collective shadow. It doesn't take much effort to get a picture of this, though it may be uncomfortable. Focus on the mission statement of any group, agency, corporation, faith community, or the character and ideals of a movement founder, and more often than not the opposite, complementary shadow is played out in how the group actually lives day to day. List the virtues of which any group or nation is proud, and the opposite, the collective shadow, will be close at hand in actual practice. I was surprised some years ago when a senior leader in a particular church group commented that he was of the opinion that the church was the worst employer he had seen. His perception was that the shadow of the public intention of the church was lived out among its own employees. Organisations that are involved in human services often exhibit a culture among the staff that is conflicted, and even abusive.

Families often have a member who stands apart, is different, and therefore seen as a problem. In my growing up years this person was often identified or self-identified as the "black sheep" of the family. I have heard more than one person wonder with some amusement if she or he wasn't mixed up with another child at birth and sent home with the wrong family. Cultures, including families, often have those who do not fit the family norms and expectations. These different ones are sometimes labelled problematic, eccentric, dreamers, free loaders, lazy or leaners. These are people who stand apart from the cultural norms of the ordinary, focused, hard-working people who support the dominant attitudes and practices of the culture. In the wider cultural scene, these outsiders also can include people who are too driven by success, too oriented to profits or wealth at any costs to others, or again they may be people who arrive in boats in distress or simply dress differently. People of faith traditions often know who is in and who is out by their standards of belief. All those who are different from the collective dominant norms represent people who may well carry the collective shadow of a culture. A specific example from times of war is the self-declared pacifist. In the past these different ones were often treated as criminals in a time when support for the war effort was needed.

The collective shadow often takes shape and is given expression through our social interactions with others. Whenever social interactions become formalised or cohesive in any context the shadow content of the group is inevitably constellated. It can be triggered by an event as simple as a person of difference moving into a previously homogenous neighbourhood. The experience of difference is a key factor in constellating the shadow in a group.

I remember as a young man in California, a Proposition being put to the vote of the state population. It had to do with fair housing, and clearly brought housing discrimination to the surface, as it had been practiced quietly in the dominant culture. In an unusual move of unity, based on commonly perceived gospel values, the leadership of the main line denominations called for the vote that would end such discrimination and open the housing market – neighbourhoods to be specific – to any, regardless of race or ethnic background. The proposition went the other way by a two to one margin. The shadow of the people spoke clearly in favour of the discriminatory practices, in spite of the long-standing claim of the nation's Pledge of Allegiance that ends, "one nation, under God, indivisible, with liberty and justice for all."

The collective or institutional shadow tends to gather together the unexamined or unconscious shadow of each of us. It is the unacknowledged shadow content that we project out onto others who are different and who carry for us the mysterious Other. The phrase we use more commonly today is "othering." It is a contemporary of the process of scapegoating. This is the raw material of which the collective shadow is constructed in the first instance. The very important truth for our ability to sustain non-violent living is that we each contribute to the common collective shadow of our culture that which we refuse to engage consciously in ourselves.

The discomfort of difference, and its attendant uncertainties, causes us to focus on very basic human needs that are activated in groups and that result in the constellation of the collective shadow. Encounter with difference often stirs up in us deep anxieties around our identity, our belonging and, ultimately, our survival. In response to these very fundamental concerns we tend to create systems and structures of security and certainty that help manage our existential anxiety. We also pursue behaviour patterns of self-interest that seek to contain our fears regarding survival.

Collectively, when our anxiety is heightened and our survival is threatened, our institutions will regress and seek new securities in tightly bounded forms and structures that take on a fundamentalist character. The nature of the fundamentalist position is to assert that there is only one way to view any issue, and it becomes critical to protect this singular point of view. The threat of difference can easily cause us to regress to an either/or approach to our circumstances. Difference, variation, complexity, ambivalence are not seen as viable ways to engage any issue. The fundamentalist stance is undertaken to protect what we know, and that we have trusted as our secure reality. This tightening of the boundaries may even extend to abandoning the founding principles and visions of the group. In the face of such heightened anxieties and fears, the group is vulnerable to accepting any ideology that promises to deliver a new protection for our anxieties and survival. In this dynamic movement, groups and institutions are as fragile as are individuals.

As a boy growing up I watched many American cowboy westerns, most of which presented the Native Americans as the dangerous Other. As settlers moved across into new lands they now claimed as their own, a classic response to an attack by the Other was the pull the wagons into a circle. That image was so common that it became a phrase in the culture and to this day there would be many who would understand its use in conversation. When danger is perceived, draw in tight and protect yourselves. It is knee jerk reaction of scapegoating that disregards a deeper analysis of the dynamic at hand and its origins. It is a violent reaction of its own kind.

We have other examples from our recent times: the Berlin Wall that kept out the "west," the wall isolating the people of Palestine in their lands within Israel, the "stop the boats" campaign in Australia, and the wall between Mexico and the United States. Whenever there is a perceived threat, real or imagined, an instinctive response often is to pull in tighter, protect what we have, and demonise the mysterious Other through attitudes and actions. These "others" carry the collective shadow of the dominant group.

The development of the collective shadow is inevitable. The psyche is nature, and the shadow is a natural aspect of the psychic life of any individual. It follows on then that when we come together in our endless forms of groups, the development of the collective shadow content is a natural consequence of our coming together. This is true of groups from sports teams to multinational corporations.

As Hollis points out in his work, over the course of the life of a group or organisation there are two developments that usually take place and that form the focus of the collective concern, even at times to eclipsing the group's, or the founding person's, original values or visions. The first is to protect the survival of the group at all costs. The second is to maintain and protect the privilege of the executive leadership, whether these are CEO's, executive management teams, professors, politicians, presidents or priests.

In the development of social institutions, a process of bureaucratisation sets in which is increasingly rigid, caught up in form, in social legitimacy, and in perpetuating the institution itself. While such collective groups may remain outwardly committed to an original purpose, internally they become increasingly unable to make the necessary changes and adaptations over time that enable them to remain faithful to their original purpose.

If an institution or any grouping of people cannot maintain a capacity to reflect critically on its life and ongoing process, it can become very destructive in some way in its corporate life. It is possible that such corporate bodies will dismiss or obstruct innovators, reformers and dissenters, inhibit and block those who would call for assessment, critique and evaluation of the performance of the corporate life, and even dehumanise others as collateral damage in the protective movement of the corporate body's present intentions.

Again, by nature, each collective group creates its own shadow. In the case of nations, each has its own dark history of bigotry, racism and the oppression of the different ones, the "less equal" others. In the nature of things it seems true that every nation, every corporate entity will employ an Other of some kind – a rival faith, a minority or different ethnic group, people who are culturally different, who speak differently, dress differently, and are of a different skin tone – the different ones on whom to project blame for whatever shortcomings, problems or inevitable changes that arise and that threaten the security of the dominant group and heighten the anxieties of its members.

Just as with the personal shadow, the collective shadow cannot be erased or dismissed. The corrective is not denial or repression. It is essential to the health of any collective group to acknowledge the potential and actual presence of this shadow. It is a reality of nature that will not go away no matter how devoted we might become in denying its reality and presence. Here the task overlaps closely with the task of each of us in our shadow work, our soul work. Collective groups and institutions are challenged to build into its systems ongoing processes that allow members to assess, critique and evaluate life together.

Our anxieties, our need to belong and to survive, all need to be honoured while we also question whether or not we need to change and adapt our paradigms and protocols in order to continue to function effectively and humanely. This involves life together in which there is honest conversation, ongoing dialogue, and an open attitude to change, adaptation and the valuing of the shared wisdom of the group. It is challenging work, and essential to an ongoing commitment to nonviolence and peacebuilding.

Institutions are necessary and natural phenomena of humans living in groups. For these to be healthy, we need to remain ready to reflect on how we are going, and to assess whether or not our original purposes, founding visions, and ideals continue as appropriate measures of our activities. It is also helpful to be quietly sceptical in the face of our ongoing confidence that we are getting it right. Complex collective groupings need to make room consciously for the reality of shadow, and to move forward carefully in attempting to be true to what has originally drawn us together.

The capacity of collective groups to undertake regular and effective reflection, and to assess the quality of their life, is directly dependent on the individuals within the group who do their individual shadow work. The challenge is to each of us to be disciplined in doing our own shadow work so that we are able to participate in the corporate conversation with conscious care and positive results.

The Golden Shadow

Is there any good news in this shadow business? Yes, indeed there is. More often than not when we engage this notion of the shadow as a lived experience, we talk of negative, problematic, shameful and violent parts of ourselves that we usually hesitate to encounter. This aspect of shadow work is essential to our own wholeness and to the well-being of any group. It is critical to do this work to sustain our intentions to live peaceful and nonviolent lives.

The other dimension of the shadow that is just as important to engage is the golden shadow. I was told that Jung once remarked that the shadow is 90% pure gold though I do not have a reference for this and no one has been able to lead me to it. The golden shadow is also part of the Other within, a part of the unlived life. It is usually a part of us that we were encouraged to set aside because it was not practical or useful to our personal development or our projected career path. Others of influence may have discouraged our following certain interests because they seemed to them to be of little significance or practical use, or perhaps beyond, or beneath, their expectations of our abilities.

The golden shadow in an individual life may appear as part of a mid-life reflection on what matters in terms of feeling more complete and whole. The golden shadow often represents a desire to connect with life differently especially if the outward path we have previously chosen has begun to feel like deadly routine and void of satisfaction. I have seen countless men in therapy return to the guitar, cooking, surfing, writing poetry or painting as ways of exploring a long buried passion or interest that offers the soul nourishment and balance and a sense of completeness. I remember working with a man in his forties who decided one year to exchange his daily five o'clock sherry with a thirty minute return to the piano which he had not touched for years. He found the practice life changing, especially in creating a gentler attitude toward life in general. I have noticed that for many women who are mothers, the movement into the realm of the golden shadow is often out from the home into the academic world for further study and qualifications, or into the work force to carve out a new sense of life and meaning in addition to the realm of mothering.

The golden shadow energy often invites us to think outside the square, to climb out of the box we have created for ourselves early in life, often at the persistent encouragement of others. A man who had been very successful in finance revealed one day his great interest in the arts and artistic expression. He realised he had taken on the life of finance to honour the sacrifices his migrant parents had made for him to make successful financial advances in life. Of the child who was drawn to the arts, he said, "I left that child alongside the road many years ago." He realised that his well being depended now on his reclaiming that child, the golden shadow, and his interest in the arts.

To access this golden shadow part of ourselves often involves being imaginative, innovative and taking risks, as we dare to try something long forgotten or never considered, and in a sense a "something" that seems to call to us, beckons us, asks for our attention, and that seems right and necessary for us now. A man in his mid-life years had a dream in which a young boy took a great and dangerous risk, and who he then had to rescue. Our shared reflections on the story led him to realise that this young boy represented his risk-taking capacity that he was famous for in his youth, but had long ago been put aside in favour of a careful and secure lifestyle. His present crisis was that he felt dried up in his corporate career and was giving fleeting consideration to becoming self-employed. Consciously he felt overwhelmed by all this, until he had the dream of the boy who took risks. In his imagination, he claimed the boy as a companion, gave him his childhood nickname, and proceeded with his help to explore and act upon the strategies that led to his being self-employed. The golden shadow often contains what we need in order to act in innovative ways to create a larger wholeness for our lives. Out of this larger sense of self who is more at peace within, we are able to engage others more fruitfully in nonviolent and peaceful ways.

Just as the negative experience of shadow has a collective aspect for us, so also does the golden shadow. In my experience, I see contemporary life in western culture as marked by an almost extreme form of individualism in so many ways. This is expressed in the ways people work, to the ways we live in our neighbourhoods. It certainly was the goal of the personal spirituality I struggled to achieve in the church of my youth. I am more and more convinced that the culture in which I live has been driven by competition and an economic notion of scarcity that causes us to see others in competitive ways rather than in cooperative relationships. I have had more than one client talk of this sense of alienation and separateness that marks his or her life in ordinary interactions. If this is so, then the golden shadow holds for us the potential to act more from a place a communal concern, care for others and a sense of connection with neighbours. Rebecca Solnit explores this side of our relationships in her work, *A Paradise Built in Hell*. It is a study of civic response to disaster, and clearly identifies the natural responses of altruism, imagination, innovation, care, concern, and communal involvements with others. Solnit's work challenges the idea that people respond communally to crisis and disaster with panic and solely out of self-interest. Her work challenges us to affirm the instinctual, natural dimensions of compassion and concern for others that are deeply rooted in our human nature. Marcus Aurelius, in his *Meditations*, asserts that, "we were made for cooperation." While individualistic pursuits and self-interest may well dominate our ordinary, conscious lives in western culture, the golden shadow is close at hand, and may often manifest quickly in times of crisis, disaster and communal need. This is an important side of human nature to affirm and claim. We have natural instincts that inspire us potentially to respond to others in crisis with care and selfless compassion.

Considering life in a collective way, whenever a group of people come together to engage a community disaster or crisis, or to consider a new approach to an issue or important matter for the community, the golden shadow is expressed in care, concern, innovation, co-learning and shared wisdom. Solnit's writing around disaster research clearly identifies these responses as instinctual, and as very much a part of our human nature. The golden shadow rises up to act when people risk their own safety to rescue others in danger. The golden shadow motivates a community to come together to sandbag a rising river, to rescue people and animals from rooftops and water covered fields in times of flooding, or to rescue people and domestic and native animals and clean up properties damaged by fierce storms and raging fires. The golden shadow inspires us to donate money, food and clothing to people struck by tragedy, and encourages us to seek to help and support the wounded, the hungry or the less able. I remember clearly several years ago when Brisbane experienced serious flooding, seeing a front-page story about how several thousands of people came out with their own brooms and tools to assist in the cleaning up of the city. It was a front-page story worth reading. Recently, the community responses to rampant fires in Australia and the winter storms in the northern hemisphere, are deeply moving examples of the golden shadow breaking through to levels of compassion, concern and sacrifice.

While these examples at times of crisis are uplifting, it is also important to give thoughtful concern for the knee jerk reactions of fear and panic in some communities that have caused the "toilet paper crisis" associated with the recent emergence globally of the coronavirus. While the golden shadow is a verifiable phenomenon, it is also true that individual anxiety for safety and survival can overwhelm us and the negative shadow of preservation can motivate some, and many, to look after only themselves, even to the point of violence. One example does not cancel out the other; again we face the complexity of who we are.

In a corporate setting, whenever an executive abandons the "lone ranger" syndrome, and turns to a team to solicit ideas and help in addressing a project or problem, the golden shadow is activated. Whenever a community or group that has long functioned in a top down manner of administration, gathers in a circle of common concern, and opens the space for shared input and collaborative interactions, the golden shadow of the group is called forth from the shared unconscious. Such events can be experienced as exciting, even sacred, as people discover each other in new ways, and find themselves embraced in a new sense of corporate identity or community.

Golden shadow, engaged in corporate settings, can breathe new life into corporate structures, bring relief to weary leaders who have too long laboured under the expectation that they must have all the answers, and extend new value to people within the system who often have the gifts, energy and wisdom to engage the ever new challenges that are a natural part of corporate endeavours. Golden shadow in the corporate setting can deconstruct the rigid patterns, forms and models of operating that no longer serve the original purpose, principles, visions and ideals of the founder or of the group. Golden shadow energy in community settings can act quickly through people to mobilise immediate care for the vulnerable, and to restore the dignity of people ravaged by crisis and loss. This golden shadow can bridge our needs for security and safety and offer new ways to engage the ever-changing, complex nature of human life. Experiences of golden shadow serve to enrich and broaden our lives. Often the experiences are fleeting or short term, yet the results for changes may be very long term. In the interests of our wholeness and our desire to live from a spirituality of nonviolence and that creates peace, it is an ongoing challenge to seek ways in which we can integrate aspects of our golden shadow into our routine, daily lives.

In a conversation with my colleague, Stacie, she put the question as to the relationship between the golden shadow and the idea of my "best" self. In a sense the two overlap, but the question invites reflection on deeper issues. The first is to realise that my "best" self may carry a heavy weight of cultural values and opinions that may or may not encourage me to develop my personal sense of myself. Who defines "best" in my life? To acknowledge the golden shadow within may be to activate and cultivate qualities, or take up interests and even passions that my family, society and faith cultures do not see as advisable or desirable. To honour the golden shadow may be to choose pacifism over military service, to choose the single life rather than marriage, to pursue a career or lifestyle in the arts rather than business, or business rather than the arts, to commit to a same sex or interracial relationship, to seek fulfilment as a person in some area of life that my various cultures will find hard to accept. My best self, when defined from within, may not look at all like the ideal images that I received throughout my younger years. The definition of best self, it seems to me, starts to take shape from within the deep and creative recesses of the individual. To be formed in the best-self images of others is to risk serious violence to me as a unique person. How I live out my ideal, or best self, from within becomes an ongoing challenge.

This leads me to another insight about Jung's work as I have experienced it from my youth. Jung's psychological model is not about social adaptation, it is about the cultivation of the individual self in the context of the larger human family. I had this conversation with my first therapist in my teenage years and it has stuck with me ever since. I am not here to fit into a predetermined cultural mould. I am here to live out my unique self in dialogue with the unconscious and in a responsible relationship with our shared life. Exploring the golden shadow, that other aspect of the mysterious Other, may well bring me into conflict with the expectations of others around me, and yet, in the long run, may enable me to make a significant contribution to our shared, common life. This would be me at my best it seems to me. Jung's psychological model does support a counter cultural attitude toward our common life at the same time appreciating that the common life is our overall, and highly valued, context.

In this chapter we have considered the reality of the shadow as first put forward by Carl Jung. We have reflected on the personal experiences of shadow, the ways in which the collective shadow is constellated and expressed, and the nature of the golden shadow for individuals and communities. What is essential to remember is that shadow work is a life-long endeavour. We do not solve shadow, we learn to live with its reality and recognise the great benefits from engaging our shadows so that we are more able to live peaceful and nonviolent lives.

CHAPTER THREE

Reflecting on Essential Matters

An image as we begin

Some years ago I was listening to a presentation on spirituality by David Tacey, the academic and scholar of Jung's work. In the course of his reflections, he drew two circles on the blackboard and in each he drew a smaller circle. David then went on to use these two circles to illustrate the change he saw in the relationship between spirituality and religion. In the first circle he labelled the larger circle "religion," and the smaller inner circle as "spirituality." In the second circle he reversed the two. The larger circle was labelled "spirituality" and the smaller inner circle was labelled "religion." The image was a visual statement of the shift that we have seen in western Christian countries in recent decades. It represents the dramatic reversal of the way many of us perceive spirituality and religion. In the world in which I grew up, spirituality was contained within the boundaries of organised religion. It was a sort of special area of the religious life for the few, sometimes defined as mystical. Today this has been turned around significantly for many people. Now spirituality is the larger framework and for some this includes alignment with an organised form of religion, but for many others it does not. I have lost count of the number of times in recent years I have heard people declare some variation of the statement that affirms that they are spiritual but do not follow any organised religion. The words will vary, but they come down to the simple affirmation: "I am spiritual, but I am not religious." A friend recently told me that this shift has become so common that it has its own acronym, NRBS – Not Religious But Spiritual.

In this third chapter of these reflections my intention is to consider what I see to be several foundational matters that influence the framework for a spirituality that will support nonviolent living. We have touched on some of these previously and will consider them again. Going over the same ground more than once is the nature of reflection on essential, or foundational, concerns. As I begin here I also want to state clearly that it is not my intention to present another set of ideals to which we might aspire. While ideals are natural to hold, they also run the risk of becoming one more "pre-fab" persona for us toward which we might strive and hope to fulfil. These matters here are meant to help us with a deeper understanding of essential elements of a nonviolent spirituality, rather than setting out ideals to try to achieve in some fixed way.

Spirituality

As we see with David Tacey's two circles, in our present day thinking and experiences, spirituality has more and more become the term we use to describe that larger realm of our spiritual discipline and experience. Alignment with an organised and clearly defined faith tradition may or may not be part of our practice and concern. Spirituality as a term here is used to encompass a wide variety of attitudes and practices.

As we enter into these reflections on the kind of spirituality that will support nonviolent living, I want to give some shape to the word, as I understand it and use it. How might we define this term and this vast, complex, intriguing, and essential dimension of our life experience?

I see spirituality constituting the framework for belief and practice that gives life meaning and purpose, and that occupies much of our thought and of our time. For me, spirituality has to do with how I perceive myself to be related to, and grounded in, a life giving energy – spirit – that is larger than myself. It has to do with how I experience and exercise my sense of connections, first to this larger spirit life, then to myself, to others near and far in the human family, and also to the entire creation. It has to do with connections. Spirituality includes the principles and values by which I live, and the practices in life that these principles and values inspire me to undertake. It includes both belief and practice. In a sense my spirituality creates for me a place in the world at every level, with myself in my time and place, with my immediate others, with the human family, and with the creation. When reflecting on life experiences or issues that arise day to day, I find it helpful to imagine where my feet are placed in the larger landscape of life. This is the image with which I began reflections in chapter one. Spirituality involves that ongoing sense of my place in a life larger than my own and how I align with this larger life. William James, in his lectures in *The Varieties of Religious Experience*, names this as the basic nature of a religious experience: acknowledging a life larger than one's own, and aligning oneself with it. Our earlier considerations of ancestors, inspiritors, and places are part of this placement of ourselves, and are integral to our spirituality. As noted, today this spirituality may or may not include a sense of being aligned with a defined religious tradition. For me, my faith tradition has been a very important part of my spiritual development, though I no longer align myself with the corporate or institutional dimensions of this tradition.

James Hollis, in his work, *Hauntings*, extends our understanding of spirituality in an interesting and unusual way. He asserts that materialistic cultures also inform and influence the development of spiritual frameworks. These influences can include technologies, seductive sexual pursuits, and endless attractive objects we feel we need, and then spend time and money collecting. Hollis also includes the notion of distractions in daily life that keep us very busy and turned away from the reflective life, and therefore, inhibit our ability to attend to relationships and concerns for more intangible matters such as identifying meaning and purpose in our lives. Hollis invites us to consider the possibility that whatever absorbs our attention day in and day out is at the core of our spirituality regardless of whether the focus is nonphysical concerns or physical objects.

The question I ask of myself concerning my spirituality is whether or not it is a distraction from myself and others, or whether is it transformative for me, and invites me into a more rich and fulfilled life within and with others, indeed with all on this planet, our shared home.

The individual

Another aspect of spirituality that is essential to our concern here is the affirmation that spirituality describes attitudes and practices that are unique to each of us. It is, therefore, more accurate to speak of spiritualties. As a result of our life histories, our place in the life journey at any given time, and the influences contained in our personal experiences, each of us will construct a framework of what we believe to be true and central to a meaningful life. It is a faith construction of how we view life, and our engagement with life. In the context of our considerations here, this faith construct is one that we both create and discover in our experiences and that will act as the framework for the practices that will serve our individual circumstances, sustain us in our living, and help us fulfil our desire to live nonviolent lives.

Our spiritualties will overlap considerably with many other persons, and also connect very little with others. Each of us must undertake the reflections necessary to identify the unique shape of our spirituality in the larger context of our relationship with life. One fact that seems important to underscore here is that we can, in some instances, be greatly helped shaping our spiritual framework through our shared life with others, and at other times it can be very unhelpful to compare our spiritual path with others. Jung says in volume two of his *Letters*, "What is healing medicine for the one, is poison for the other." My observations over time lead me to conclude that, more often than not, when we compare ourselves with others, we lose! Our spiritualties are highly individual and it is a significant challenge for each of us to undertake identifying what are our principles for living and the actual practices that we need to undertake in fidelity to these principles. While our spiritual frameworks may overlap with others, it is important for us to give individual shape to our framework in our own words and in conscious awareness of our own needs, desires and hopes for life.

This challenge to each of us is made more complex in that

our spiritual framework and practices will, of necessity, change as life continues to unfold. The spiritual framework and practices of my life in my twenties are significantly different from the framework and practices by which I am trying to live now as a man in my seventies. Some beliefs and practices have remained constant, while others have changed many times over as life has unfolded and brought me wonderful moments, satisfying achievements, embarrassing failures, difficult and painful times, predictable results of my labour, and many unexpected joys and challenges. Exercising the freedom and responsibility to make changes is an ongoing task. This ongoing task takes place in the wider reality of my life in community.

The community

Having affirmed the personal nature of our individual spiritualties, I want also to affirm the continual movement between us as individuals and our community, or communities. So, we come again to the experience of community. Community is the larger framework in which I develop and hold to my beliefs and then live out my spiritual practices. It is the community to which I make my contributions from the unique person that I am. Having been nurtured in my early years in a very individual sense of religious practice, I have come more and more to understand and affirm the community as the primary, wider, fundamental reality in which I live out my life. This is a statement of the obvious, but one that is important to affirm as it represents a significant shift from the approach to spirituality that shaped me as a young man. In my growing up years in my faith tradition the emphasis was certainly on the individual life, personal religion, and often the community was given secondary consideration at best. These days I see my individual life and my community life as an endless dance between self and other.

Without the various layers and levels of community in which I live, my life really has no significance or meaning, and I certainly cannot sustain my life apart from the communities in which I share. At the core I am a communal person. Affirming the community as the wider and essential context for our living is a critically important undertaking in our times. I am encouraged to hear more and more the reaffirmation of the solidarity of humankind as we engage the global issues of our future. Recently the phrase "the common good" has begun to surface again as an image that helps us consider what is best for the wider community. For me, this represents an important shift in our collective consciousness. From the work of Desmond Tutu I have become aware of the term "Ubuntu," variously translated "I am because we are." The motto, "Better together," forms a foundation of the work of Australian-South African photographer and filmmaker, Adrian Steirn.

In section one I considered briefly the various levels of community in which I participate, including giving thought to the ongoing dialogue with creation. As well as reflecting on our somewhat awesome and mysterious oneness as a human family, I continue to be touched deeply with the deep truth or our oneness, our communion with creation, with nature. It is both exciting and challenging to affirm that I am connected to, a part of, and an inhabitant with, all others on the planet, and I am a participant in our shared life by virtue of my birth. I am challenged and intrigued to consider how my psychological self as an independent unique creation, actually stands in the larger framework of my ecological self, the "I am" that is inextricably and intimately linked to the entire creation. In his work, *Ecological Intelligence*, Ian McCallum, asserts over and over again that we are the human animals in the fabric of creation and that our survival depends on the health and well being of all of creation on the planet.

Recently I viewed a brief online video on the National Geographic website. It was about emerging explorers being funded by the National Geographic. While some of these persons were briefly featured in the video, this line was included as a voice over: "The future of exploration is finding out where humans fit among all the other species." We are invited to imagine the creation of all species and see where we now fit in with all others, rather than assuming that we are at the top of the stack and somehow separate from all others. The movement in our time that is essential is from an anthropocentric to a biocentric understanding of all creation. We humans are in the mix and very dependent on the entirety of creation for our existence. We are one, large, vast, mysterious and marvellous community.

Likewise, while viewing on the internet some work by Adrian Steirn, I read his simple assertion that "What we do to the animals, we do to ourselves." We are invited to see ourselves as an integral part of the entire community of creation. There is truth in saying that to abuse the creation is to abuse ourselves.

In specific terms of humanity, I am part of the one entire family and we are linked in a complex, remarkable, planetary human community. The long revered poetic image that we are all brothers and sisters affirms this great truth that is crucial to living a nonviolent life with each other. While the images of brothers and sisters is more common, Desmond and Mpho Tutu in their work, *The Book of Forgiving*, affirm that we are all cousins, since we have emerged from the ancient human line in Africa thousands of years ago. These word maps and images present a tremendous challenge that is both exciting and unnerving.

Ten years ago, when I created the statements that became my personal principles, I included the affirmation, "All humanity is my family; I was born into community." We will look at the principles in chapter five. The focus over these years has been the human family, and I have found that this truth can stretch my consciousness. At times it is uncomfortable. I am continually challenged to affirm and I try to sustain a global perspective of human interconnectedness. My local and personal communities exist in this global context, and these more local loyalties must be assessed for their claims on us in this wider global framework. In the face of our assertion that we all are one family, it becomes very difficult to objectify, degrade and dismiss others as being less than we are. Violence against each other becomes harder to justify and to enact. The reality of our being one human family challenges me to seek relationships at all levels of community that are life affirming, supportive of others and nonviolent.

As I reflect on the lively dynamic of community, it is important for me to recall over and over again these various levels of community in which I do live and on which I depend: planet, nation, state, and neighbourhood. How do I step up to more thoughtful and caring relationships with all of creation and the people in these global, national and local groups, communities? The challenges continue, and finally I come down to the community of my friends and close loved ones, who, along with my ancestors, contribute much to the shape of the life I live, and the spiritual framework that I hold as mine. At every level of community, I am invited to see myself as living in the midst of several communities that are critical to my life and wellbeing. In the face of our oneness as a human family, I am invited to acknowledge a deep sense of gratitude to many others, some known and others mostly unknown, for my life, and to take my share of responsibility in promoting the health and wellbeing of all of us and all that is.

Inspired and instructed by the insights of many, I affirm that I do not create these communities, but have shared in one or more of them from the day of my birth. I was born into community. Community is a given, a gift that comes with life. I cannot build community as much as to be present to creation, and to humanity, and let community embrace me and teach me about myself and how we are meant to be with each other. I see more and more clearly that this takes time, mutual respect, and a commitment to be open to others in the midst our differences.

In recent years I have had the privilege of sharing in two small communities. One has been a men's book study, and the other has been a Community of Practice for Daily Nonviolent Living. Each met monthly; the men's book study continues, while the Community of Practice has ended. Over time we experienced a deepening of community as we shared together. The book study focuses on our ongoing learning from writers whose thoughts we find helpful. The other centred on stories of violent and non-violent moments in our daily lives that we shared to encourage each other in the ongoing task of choosing the way of nonviolent living. Silence, relaxed sharing, attentive listening, deep reflections, mutual respect and laughter all contribute to the deepening of these communities of co-learning and shared wisdom. We have been present with each other, and community has shaped us.

In the light of more recent thought, I want now to look at this from a different perspective. In the movement between the community and the individual, I have long held to a developmental model that involves moving from being shaped by others to shaping ourselves. We grow up in life being a person who is largely shaped by our various communities. I refer to this as being a referential person. In our growing up we move more and more to being a person who shapes life and identity from within, that is to becoming a self-referential person. Recently, as I read a brief forward by James Hillman entitled, "A Psyche the Size of the Earth," in the collection of essays, *Ecopsychology*, I found myself challenged to amend this simple two-phase movement, the referential to self-referential person.

In interpreting Hillman's thinking into my life, the developmental movements become three, and go something like this. First, I began my life as a referential person. At the beginning I had no conscious sense of being separate from others, and as I became aware of this, I still took my cues from others as to how I was to be in the world. Family, culture and faith traditions all informed me as to who I am and how I am to be in this human adventure. I was raised up to believe and to act in certain ways. I was shaped from the outside. This is the dominant movement of development when young. As a grandfather I am presently watching my young grandson go through the same process.

A second and essential movement arises in this growing up time, quietly at first, but relentless in its desire to be engaged. It is the sense of "I" from within. What do *I* think, what do *I* believe, how will *I* act? It is the beginning of a self-referential point of view about my life. The separation from others begins to happen and grows naturally. A movement begins between two points of view, simply stated as self and other. It becomes that life-long dance between the two – the individual and the community. A goal in this is to become a self-referential person. It is to know where I end and others begin. It is to have boundaries between self and other. It is to claim my own truth, my point of view and my chosen path of action. In countless ways the self-other interaction continues all through life, sometimes slowly and easily, and at other times dramatically and swiftly. In the midst of the others, family, culture, and faith traditions, I discover and hold to my own ground in dynamic interaction. Sometimes I align myself contentedly with others. At other times I stand alone with determination, even defiance. I belong and I do not belong. At times I am settled in my culture, and at others I am decidedly counter-cultural.

Hillman and many others now challenge me to extend this view to a third movement or phase of conscious experience. It is to become referential once again as I grow to understand the world of Other as the larger context for my individual, self-referential life. Like the wandering hero, I return home to the people and bring my individual gifts, my individual life experiences, and my individual reflections on life, and these I contribute to the people – to my People – for the common good.

This expanding consciousness goes further in our time. The boundaries around self soften now to include Other in the broadest sense. Other includes all of life on our island home, this planet earth. My soul now sits referentially in the larger, lively context of the world soul. As we have considered, other people become neighbours, brothers, sisters, cousins. Plants and animals become family – soul family. Gandhi asserted, "All is one." This is the truth into which we grow, into which we surrender ourselves and come to rest. We continue to dance between our unique self and the other, with a deeper understanding and appreciation for our interdependence, with each other and with the creation. Ancient wisdom declares that the soul is larger than the body; there is the world soul – anima mundi – in which I live, on which I depend. What happens to my earth family, to my brothers, sisters and cousins has a direct impact on me. To abuse the earth, to savage the landscape, is to do violence to my soul. To abuse other people, neighbours, sisters, brothers, is to violate myself. There is one soul, world soul, in which my unique individual expression of life and soul are embedded and to which I am inextricably linked.

In the Christian writings of Paul we read that if one suffers, all suffer, if one rejoices all rejoice. Hafiz the Sufi poet tells us there is only one body we can wound when we strike out in rage. Hafiz names it as the Christ. John Donne told his readers that the bell, when it tolls, tolls for us all. As we have considered in the first chapter, the dynamic that operates daily in this world-soul life is dialogue, an endless, two-way communication between our individual souls and the world soul.

This three part process that Hillman identifies, which is complex and mixed in our actual living, now invites us to consider that the mature self is no longer the individual, autonomous self apart from the Other. I referred earlier to the ecological self, and this, the "global self," now can represent for us the deeper maturity of the individual who finds her or his life's purpose and meaning within the larger community of humans, in an appropriate relationship to all other species and within the entire creation. At the core of our being we are persons within communities in the deepest sense. Influenced by Hillman's reflections, I have now changed the statement in my principles to read, "All creation is my family; I was born into community."

Differences

It seems clear that diversity makes for a healthy environment. When we reflect on the individual engaged in the eternal dance with community, the challenge that emerges is to make room for difference. Diversity has the potential to enrich us, and it also can at times cause us discomfort, anxiety and anger. Our Pace e Bene Constitution includes the phrase, "rejoicing in our differences ..." Whenever I read this I can't help but have a bit of a laugh. Who does that, rejoices? Well, I do at times and in certain instances, but there are times when making room for difference is a substantial, and annoying, challenge.

Questions arise for me over and over again. "What is it about difference that is so unnerving? With how much difference can I cope? This second question was behind a conference I facilitated years ago wherein a group of us considered our relationship to our dominant culture. The distinction from dominant culture was heightened by the fact that the conference was held over New Year's Eve and New Year's Day. In the past year I made a poster with a question about engaging difference. The design is a large, colourful question mark down the right side of the poster. These words flow down the left side of the poster. "How much difference am I willing to tolerate, endure, accept, welcome, encourage, embrace, celebrate?"

Celebrating differences invites me to be firm at the core and adaptable at the edges. This is sometimes a risk when I encounter differences that touch on my passions or core values. Most of the time I do well enough dealing with differences in apparel, body decoration, skin tone, and with most cultures. That said, I continue to struggle to understand people who hold to conflicting political points of view, or who work hard to achieve a lifestyle that I don't get, who are dismissive of matters that are important to me, or who condone aggressive or violent solutions to conflicts without any consideration of alternatives. This struggle just never seems to go away. A day out shopping at a mall can bring up the issue of difference as I navigate through and around others.

One issue that emerges as part of this involves the limits of my understanding. Engaging people who are different, or hold to different points of view, challenges me to listen in carefully to those others, and reminds me that I do not know it all. In my personal principles there is the phrase, "There are many truths I do not know." To own this can variously create anxiety and/or relief. When I encounter difference, my safe and secure worldview, my dearly held points of view, can be shaken and I sometimes must acknowledge my rising anger. I am learning over time to hold this awareness consciously, to ride with this and to learn as I go how to respond and act. I have some understanding as to why people can get agitated to the point of becoming violent in defending a heartfelt point of view. There is one in my village who rages from time to time.

When I was a young man, an older man with whom I worked said to me one day, "You know, George, the older I get the less I know for sure." I nodded in some silent way, wondering what was wrong with him. I was young, successful and I knew! Now I remember him with affection and a quiet smile. I get it … now. I can talk easily about adaptable edges, but I realise there is an ongoing anxiety in engaging differences, and perhaps having to amend my point of view to include others or to learn from them.

The world in which I grew up seems now far more set in expectations for young people. Sameness seemed to be a norm to both desire and my expectations for the future. I well remember the saying, "Birds of a feather flock together." In my world it had serious racial overtones, but it also implied that it was best to stay with your own kind in terms of faith tradition, social pursuits, gender roles and long-term values for life. Like-minded was best. Difference was okay as long as it was not too different. The shadow side of this was a quiet dismissal and fear of the "Other" in a variety of forms. I see now the subtle violence in all of this woven into my growing up years.

In a time of an ongoing emerging global consciousness, I conclude that our lives depend on a radical change toward the inclusive global community – radical inclusivity. My at home learning began with my wife, Shirley, years ago. She was very extraverted, a major attraction for me, and I am very introverted. Early on we had to learn to cope with these differences day to day, and I had to realise that I was a better person for engaging with life as she experienced and lived it. I learned over time it was the same for her. We often would comment that appreciating these daily differences between us saved our marriage. Without her now I have to be the extravert for myself, and that is a challenge in its own right. I recognise her influence whenever I do, or say, something much like she would have done or said. I suppose that this sounds like a simple enough experience, yet Jung says somewhere that the simple things are often the hardest. To be confronted with the challenge of difference in my daily life in the most routine and intimate ways certainly drove the lesson home. It reminds me of the stone thrown in the pond and the ripples that move out from the centre point of impact. I see it as something like that.

The challenge of difference ramps up to a serious level when I accept human solidarity as essential to our future on this planet, and now try to cope with differences that are in opposition or are adversarial to my points of view. Shadow projections can happen in these instances in a flash, and I am often brought down a peg or two in my delusion of righteousness as I ponder how to imagine oneness, solidarity, with those with whom I differ deeply.

It only leaves me caught in confusion when I think of those at the far end of the continuum whose actions toward others can only be described as evil. I will stand against such behaviours, but am challenged to remember that those who hold them are also members of the one human family. Gandhi reminds us that all life is one. Some call us brothers and sisters. Desmond and Mpho Tutu, invite us to see that we are all cousins up to ten thousand times removed. One, we are one, and this extends to all life on the planet as well. We will revisit this later.

Much of this reflection deals with relationships outside us, from family to the global family. An equal challenge is to learn to celebrate the amazing differences that we find intra-psychically. Here we come again to the image of the village, and connect again with the personal shadow. The scope of the villagers within is an ongoing source of amazement to me. How is it I can be both generous and selfish? How is it that I can be both courageous and fearful? How has it come about that I have the capacities to be vengeful and forgiving? How is it that I am able to be compassionate and warm hearted and so coldly judgemental? Years ago a theologian I deeply admired referred to this inner world of ours as his zoo! This seemed more appropriate to explain to himself the diversity he experienced in his own soul. I sometimes feel zoo-like.

There are times when I am not sure whether to be fascinated or horrified at the breadth of diversity in my village. I also find this true of the lives and souls of the people with whom I share intimate soul stories. More than once I have had a male client admit that he had no desire to know what was on the other side of "that" door, even if the door was slightly ajar in invitation. One man laughed to admit that, in his imagination, he put his hand around the partly open door to see if he could feel anything in that darkened room. Another just said, "I am not sure I want to know who is there." A bit of fear is an understandable response to the mystery of our souls.

At times I shake my head in wonder at the complexity of the human personality. To include in my self-understanding and my landscape of the world the vast spectrum of differences among us and within me, is sometimes just plain hard work. Hard work though it be, rejoicing in differences, celebrating our diversity, inner and outer, is essential to a spiritual framework what will sustain peace building and nonviolent living.

Violence

What to say? We are surrounded by experiences of violence on every level. Internally we beat up on ourselves. I certainly know the experience of an interior civil war between opposing points of view. We see violence in close relationships, in our cultures, social structures, and political systems. We experience violence in cultures of industries, policies attempting to help those in need, and in faith traditions, where it is often made clear who is in and who, therefore, is out. It surrounds us and is woven into the tapestries of our cultural, national and faith histories. And it is very much in me, and my lived experience. I know violence well in my story, and this is why I spend time reflecting on the character of a nonviolent spirituality. These reflections, whatever else they are, represent an attempt to address, to respond to, the violence that is a significant part of my story and my responses to life.

From where I observe life, within me and around me, I affirm that the capacity for violence is simply a part of our complex human nature. For me, to deny this is set myself up for an endless civil war within my soul that will only create more violence toward myself, and this feral violence has the potential to get projected out onto others. While I do not have final answers to the mysteries of human nature and to the presence of violence in us, what I know is that I need a framework that helps me engage creatively, and hold responsibly, my capacity for violence.

In the soul work that I do, I realise that many of us tend to deal with this capacity for violence by exclusion. I would suggest that it is the training we receive from our dominant cultures of family, faith traditions and cultures. We learn to avoid, deny, push away, repress, and suppress those uprisings of violent energies. This capacity for violence is something of which we learn to be ashamed and embarrassed, and by which we are humiliated when it erupts into life. This capacity in most of us resides in what we have considered as the mysterious Other, or Shadow, in chapter two. More than one person has expressed to me a strong desire to have it gone, taken away, stamped out, expelled from life. My observations lead me to conclude that these attitudes or wishes of exclusion, do not work; it certainly does not work for me. As one writer affirmed, what is pushed away does not go away. For me, this is a critical point: exclusion does not work in addressing our capacity for violence.

Violence is a part of our human nature and we need a spiritual framework that assists us in dealing wisely with this lived experience when it arises. Part of our dealing with violence is to reflect more deeply on the possibility that violent impulses – angers, rages and impulses to do harm – at least on a personal level, may at times be responses to life that contain opportunities for positive, personal insight and learning. When I find anger rising it helps greatly to regroup and quiz myself. What has set me off into rage? Who in my village responds with anger at this situation?

What does my angry response say about me? These, and others, are useful questions. It is also possible that group responses of violence, while potentially tragic, may hold within them opportunities to understand more deeply the lives and circumstances of those who protest. I keep reminding myself that conscious self-reflection is an essential trait to being human.

While some of my responses of anger may be due to my shadow being twigged or exposed, it is also true that personal expressions of anger, and collective expressions as well, may very well be the rising up of a life energy that affirms our existence and dignity against a perceived threat. I read somewhere along the way that anger is one way of saying, "I am here!" It is not unusual for people to respond with anger when they do not feel heard, or experience that they are being ignored, dismissed, excluded or not taken seriously. It is not unusual for people to erupt with anger when their worldview is threatened, or their economic and social stability is called into question. It is not at all unusual for people to respond with anger when they feel demeaned for some aspect of their being that is beyond their choice, such as gender, skin colour or sexual orientation. In these and many instances our angers and rages may well be highly energised eruptions that proclaim our existence, our dignity and our entitlement to basic respect as human beings. These violent upsurges may well be forms of self-affirmation that enable us to stand firmly for ourselves and others when we are faced with experiences and actions that appear threatening, unjust and demeaning. In this sense these violent moments may be interpreted as positive for the individual and the group. How these moments are processed is another matter that requires our ongoing, careful attention. Acknowledging our angers and rages is the first step in determining how to harness the energy and transform it into creative and nonviolent responses that build peace. From where I am placed, this is a critical shift of consciousness for nonviolent and peace creating individuals and groups. How do I/we shift the energy from our experiences of wounding to a creative, strategic energy that will open pathways for the processes of peace building? My experiences have been that the shift requires me to acknowledge the wounding and the feelings that go with being victimised, and then to reclaim agency in my life and create an assertive response. I have not always been successful, but looking back over many years, I see the importance of having this as an overall intention and response. Remaining a victim will not heal me; finding a nonviolent way forward does much to promote healing for me and for others.

Coming at this from another point of view, I can affirm that there are experiences that may feel violent to us, but are intended to be for our healing and wellbeing. In medical circumstances, procedures including chemotherapy, invasive surgeries and simple wound repairs may be painful and feel like an assault in the short term, but in the long term they are positive for us. This was certainly my experience in undergoing open-heart bypass surgery. The experience was an invasive assault on my body that also saved my life. I am grateful to be alive, but also realise how extensive that invasive experience was and how long it took me to recover on both physical and psychic levels.

Likewise we may experience a blunt opinion from a family member, colleague or boss at work as a violent assault on our dignity, yet this may be the very wakeup call we need to change our behaviour and realign our lives with our own deeper truth and character. It may also be a signal that we are involved in a situation that is not life giving, and requires us to look for another place to be. A nightmare dream or fantasy may wake us with a start, and a pounding heart, and yet on reflection be the very input we need to consider more carefully how we are living. I remember well the dream I had in 1977, of my pending castration, that led me into deeper reflective and analytical work, and became the initiation into the work I now engage with deep passion and gratitude. These are examples of violence in the service of a larger good.

These experiences may inhabit our lives under other labels – depression, breakdown, redundancy, facing into sobriety, loss in relationship, missing out on a promotion. While experienced as violent assaults on the present status quo of our lives, they often become the initiatory experiences that serve us well in engaging a new way to live. In these and many other experiences that seem violent at the time, we can come to understand that the intent is to heal and encourage us forward positively in our lives. I remember well in my late teens asking for help from a mentor to solve quickly a financial problem that I had created for myself, by loaning me the money to resolve the issue. He refused flatly and I was shocked. I was hurt and felt rejected. He then offered me a possible plan and the assurance that he would stand behind me if I would undertake to act on it. I did, it was successful in a longer term, and I have never forgotten the importance of having sorted out with discipline the mess I had created.

There is much more to consider in our reflections on violence – volumes exist to help us with this. My intention here is to state the obvious presence of violence in our lives in relation to these reflections, and to try to move past a simplistic point of view that would render all violence as negative in value. However I engage the complex nature of violence, I need a spiritual framework that will help me discern the nature of my angers, rages, and violent urges when they arise, so that I can determine how to respond to them, and how to use the energies in creative and life-giving ways. It is not life giving or helpful to make futile attempts to deny and banish anger, rage and violence from my life in the pursuit of a more positive spiritual pathway. Ultimately my human nature will not allow this, and the violent impulses of the soul will continue regardless of what position I adopt toward them. It seems denial does not work, so engagement, painful as it is, is the better option.

Another question that I ponder in this regard has to do with my human nature and the cultures in which I have lived and which have helped shape me. I conclude that aspects of my cultures – family, faith and society – in many ways have cultivated violent attitudes and opinions in me through values of exclusion and superiority that are seen as normal. At the same time aspects of my cultures – family, faith and society – have given me significant assistance in dealing with my human nature and handling my violent responses with care. Both are true. What I have taken from this is to look with a critical eye at these cultural environments and to choose consciously and intentionally those values that support nonviolence as I understand it. In some ways it has led me to value counter-cultural attitudes that focus differently than the dominant culture. To a significant extent we are, by nature, complex, and an ongoing mystery to ourselves. I know myself to have the capacity for violence by nature, now, how will my spiritual framework serve me to engage myself as I am, so that I may live at peace with myself and to build peace with others? This is an ongoing question for me, not so much to answer but in which to live and on which to reflect. Engaging our complexities as honestly as we can is critical to creating a nonviolent, peace-making framework. It is a never-ending work in progress inviting continual, even daily reflection.

Spirit

These very unfinished reflections on violence draw me now into equally unfinished reflections on Spirit. At present, Spirit is the word I use most comfortably for God and/or divinity. This great reality is shrouded in mystery, and is characterised by paradox and complexity. I remember attending a conference on mystery in 1975 at Grace Cathedral in San Francisco at which Dr. Margaret Mead asserted that engaging God includes engaging the never to be known. Mystery is at the core of this relationship. For me, Spirit, while mystery, is also immediate to our daily experiences and is essential to our considerations of violence and a spirituality that will sustain a nonviolent and peace creating way of life.

About this Spirit business I find myself deeply involved in yet another ongoing work in progress; it seems to be a lifelong reflection. In the face of the mystery of Spirit, I consider simple and definitive answers with a bit of suspicion. Having said this, I intend to wade into murky waters and hope for the best.

I have come to see Spirit as the energised reality, the life force, of all that is, and all that animates life. I have also come to conclude that Faith traditions attribute both personal imagery and complex values to this Spirit energy in positive and negative aspects, and categorise Spirit expressions in this way. Yet in my opinion Spirit is ultimately One; Spirit is Spirit. I also observe in my lived experience that it takes ongoing discernment and wise counsel to contend with the divisions we create in an attempt to engage with, and cope with, Spirit. We meet Spirit in an amazing and endless variety of ways. At times in our personal experience Spirit comes to us in quiet and consoling ways, at other times Spirit is manifest in ways that are challenging, difficult, even overwhelming and perceived negatively as violent.

It seems it is we who must determine which manifestation is holy or unholy, good or evil.

As I have considered Carl Jung's work over the years, I conclude that he challenges us to see that Spirit at the core is One, and it is we who must make the necessary choices to determine whether the Spirit energy is used for good or ill. This places a high stake on our human consciousness and free will to decide. I have long held that Jung holds to a very high opinion of humanity and the crucial nature of human consciousness. With this positive opinion of us comes enormous responsibility for our actions and for the well-being of all creation.

From this point of view it seems true to affirm again that expressions of spirit that are violent and threatening may actually hold the seeds to our healing and well-being. It is also true to affirm the opposite, that experiences we welcome that are gentle, warm and consoling, may well lead to our undoing. In our consideration of nonviolent spiritualities, we find that our understandings of Spirit and violence are deeply complex, and these important experiences must be addressed with careful discernment at every turn. Human consciousness is a key factor in how we engage with Spirit.

Yet, while this point of view makes sense for me to a degree, it also causes me some discomfort. The implication here is that Spirit is neutral and passive, and even indifferent, and we humans are the key in determining the nature of the encounter. Somewhere in this there is some sense of truth for me, but it is also true that I do not experience Spirit as simply passive. There is another experience that is also true. In the first chapter I reflected on the nature of Dialogue, and here again it becomes important in our considerations.

One of the most significant experiences of my life has been to engage, symbolically, the dreams of the night, half awake fantasies of middle night, and the drifting fantasies of the daydreaming many of us seem to do. The dreams, these symbolic stories, have been my companion, and a faithful resource, now for over sixty years. I treasure their guidance, their insight and the gentle, and not so gentle ways, in which these stories have consoled me, challenged me, terrified me, warned me and confirmed my chosen path. They, too, are of Spirit, and I do not make, design or control them. In fact their great value is that I do not. In this instance it is Spirit that takes the initiative that acts upon me. The dream is the Spirit speaking into our dialogue.

The questions come rushing in. What is this Spirit that creates these stories for us — tailor made for each of us — night after night? Here is Spirit that, or who, initiates, provokes, takes the lead in order to correct the path, and above all seems to have our best interests in mind. Among some people of faith there is talk questioning the notion of the interventionist God. What do we make of this active, initiating, intervening Spirit of dialogue? What do we make of the Spirit that, or who, embraces the writer and the words flow, who overtakes the composer and the notes arrange themselves, or so it seems? What have we to say to the painter who senses herself a conduit or channel for the way in which the paint arrives on the canvas? And if this Spirit is a life giving and healing Spirit, a Spirit for good, what do we make of the Spirit that tends at other times to overwhelm us and to enact destructive violence on so many levels of our experiences?

Regardless of how we conceive this, we have two truths sitting side by side. First, our human consciousness is essential to determining how Spirit energy is interpreted, given value and expressed. Second, Spirit initiates, we receive Spirit, we are acted upon and it can be for good and for ill. In one sense we have control, and in another we seem to have little, if any. In both instances we can benefit from Spirit, or suffer its presence and get caught up in overwhelming experiences. Such is the mysterious reality of Spirit for me as I reflect at this time in my life.

I am foolish to believe that I might tidy this up neatly. The broodings on the mystery of Spirit continue, and are important to our exploration of spiritualities that will support our desire to live nonviolent lives. An important outcome of these reflections for me has been the deeper realisation that this attitude toward Spirit allows me to make room for others who experience Spirit differently. Rather than be caught up in conflicts between differing points of view or faith traditions, this perspective invites us to drop down to the common desire of all humanity to find ways to engage Spirit in our vast and mysterious world. Beneath our differences we are all searching for ways to create safe places for ourselves in this fascinating, frightening and wondrous world. We have had remarkable historical figures who have embodied this Spirit at various times and places, around whom we have built frameworks and traditions that have provided countless peoples with meaningful ways to engage the mystery of our human experience. Coming to this place of deeper common ground enhances my capacity to engage with respect and reverence those who interpret and assign value and create meaning in very different frameworks and images. Creating spaces for other searching hearts, rather than having the right answers for us all, enlarges my capacity for wonder and for creating peaceful ways with others.

I am drawn to this excerpt from a poem by Meister Eckhart as translated by Daniel Ladinsky in the collection from various traditions, *Love Poems from God*: "All language has taken an oath to fail to describe Him; any attempt to do so is the height of arrogance and will always declare some kind of war: the inner ones that undermine our strength, and the outer ones conflicts that maim red." Spirit, it is the great mystery.

We have thus far reflected briefly on several matters that will inform our considerations of nonviolent spiritualities. These include definitions of spirituality, the importance of the individual, our participation in communities, the reality of our differences, the complexities of violence and the mystery of Spirit. Using what we have thus far considered as an overall framework, in the next chapter we will look more deeply at several characteristics that help us shape a nonviolent spiritual framework for our living.

CHAPTER FOUR

Characteristics of a Nonviolent Spirituality

Thus far we have reflected on our sense of place and the task of knowing ourselves in reference to a nonviolent spiritual framework. We have considered the mysterious Other – the experience of the shadow, both personal, collective and golden. We have also looked briefly at matters that, for me, are essential to a foundation for nonviolent peacebuilding. In this chapter I intend to consider some specific characteristics of, and resources for, this nonviolent spiritual framework. Some subjects I consider here will have been touched on previously. Walking around in this soulful landscape risks repetition as well as considering matters from different perspectives. I hope this can be useful in helping us to ground the essential concepts and practices more deeply.

A Starting place

At times in my own broodings over the years I have begun with a negative approach, that is, I begin by stating clearly what something is not. In this instance there are three characteristics often associated with spiritualities that I highlight here. These can contribute to attitudes and behaviours that often result in violence toward ourselves and toward others. It is important to identify these, as I see them as widespread and unhelpful in developing a framework that sustains nonviolent living.

The first is the notion of purity. The notion of purity here refers to a mindset that seeks to be free of any thoughts and attitudes that we have been schooled to see as negative, selfish, weak, socially unacceptable, or even evil. Simply put, we are often schooled to deny the land of the mysterious Other, the Shadow. The image of purity has to do with a flawless state of being. The desire for purity requires us somehow to clear out, to get rid of, and to push away those attitudes and characteristics that are actually part of our nature, but that we have been encouraged to see as impure and undesirable. Too often this approach divides us against ourselves and contributes to what can only be seen as a long-term civil war in the soul. Purity as a goal leads to a spiritual framework that invites us to feel shame and guilt, and to hide away parts of us from others as well as ourselves. It is a spiritual framework characterised by dismissal, denial and suppression, and such attempts in the interests of nonviolent spiritual growth are futile, for eventually our nature will not be denied.

The second is the striving to be perfect. While it is true that the soul needs images and notions of ideals, it is also true that we need to be clear that in life as we experience and live it, these are goals we will not reach. In my tradition the teaching attributed to Jesus in the Gospel of Matthew, 5:48, that calls us to perfection is seriously misleading. Translating the Greek word, *telios*, as "perfection," is an unfortunate interpretation. This Greek word is more accurately translated as "completion" or "wholeness." The teaching challenges us to seek the completion or wholeness of our lives, not our perfection. Perfection in our common understanding again requires denial and exclusion. We seek to be perfect by getting rid of parts of who we are by nature.

Many years ago I was conversing with a woman of my faith tradition who had come to a place of feeling quite settled within herself. She spoke softly in a way that seemed to her to be the tone and volume of one who was grounded in a solid spiritual sense of peace. She then went on to explain that she had one ongoing agitation. She verbally described the image. It was like having a little person sitting on her shoulder criticising her. I asked her what she wanted to do about this and she suddenly turned to her own shoulder and yelled, "Get outa here!" It was a startling eruption of a passionate energy, and revealed that, in her understanding, the only hope for spiritual maturity or perfection was to get rid of this annoying little person on her shoulder. This is perfection by exclusion.

The third characteristic is that of dualism, that is, black or white, either/or thinking. I am either this OR that. In this model there is no grey. A colleague once remarked that this point of view is infantile at best. In most every instance, this framework sets us up for that ongoing civil war.

Much of this futile civil war takes us again to the realm of the mysterious Other, the Shadow aspect of personality. My lived experience leads me to affirm that what is pushed away will not go away. Attitudes and feelings that we wish to beat into submission, destroy, banish or escape, when pushed away, simply sink back into the unconscious, there to roam freely. These aspects of us we refuse to acknowledge and engage will re-appear wherever a crack is found in our carefully constructed social persona. This repressed shadow energy emerges as a slip of the tongue here, a raised eyebrow there, a wisecrack, a smirk and/or shrug of the shoulders in another instance. It may be a subtle looking away from an unpleasant scene or person. It might be as dramatic as a sudden violent, judgemental expression or an explosion of an opinion that is "out of character," such that we express our own wonder and say, "I don't know what came over me." The repressed shadow lives and we are at civil war within.

Somewhere tucked away in the heart of this exclusive spiritual framework is the myth of redemptive violence, wherein we believe that we must hate and annihilate the unsavoury parts of ourselves and make no compromise with evil. We do violence to ourselves in order to be redeemed, to be perfect. This, of course, sets us on a path of legitimising violence toward any others onto whom we project the unsavoury Other, the shadow. If we insist on standards of purity and perfection that succeed by exclusion, and assess our world in either/or categories of thought, we set ourselves up at some point and in some way to defend and justify violent behaviours and thoughts toward ourselves an others. The histories of many faith traditions are scarred with examples of this tragic process of negative projection.

In my experience over many years, I conclude that many people of my own Christian faith tradition are still schooled in a spirituality that can lead to self-hatred, loathing, shame, remorse and guilt. We are held to a code of purity that is offended by impure thoughts, especially sexual fantasies, or fantasies of angry outbursts, violence, retaliation, or revenge. We are trained to seek perfection by exclusion, by getting rid of that which contradicts our chosen path of belief, or offends our ideal images. We are encouraged to judge others and ourselves in either/or categories, and to believe that troublesome and negative thoughts and experiences have no meaning, no value, and no purpose. These impure, shameful and offensive parts of ourselves have nothing to teach us, and our good standing with God requires us to rid ourselves of such hateful feelings, attitudes and behaviours. Having now identified these three problematic qualities that can undermine our efforts to develop a spiritual framework that will sustain our intentions to live nonviolent lives, I intend to consider characteristics that I have found essential to my efforts and hopes in living a life committed to nonviolent peace making.

Reconciliation

A nonviolent spiritual framework that will support our intentions for peace work is centred on reconciliation. It is an attitude that supports practices that seek restoration and integration. An image for this spiritual framework is the act of gathering in, of welcoming in all who come. Gathering as a movement seeks to bring together people and ideas. The work begins within. In my inner village the gathering in takes place in a circle that is surrounded by the dwellings of the villagers. In the centre of the gathering circle is a tall tree that provides a canopy of shelter. The circle, an ancient image, affirms a sense of equality among the gathered, and provides a central setting in which all can be seen, valued and heard. The reconciling nature of this spiritual framework extends outwardly as well. The image of the gathering in of others expresses a fundamental commitment to hospitality. I have found it challenging and helpful to ask myself how I can be person of hospitality not only in my actions, but also in my very being and presence. How can I offer, or contribute to, a gathering space in my very person when with others? The mental image of standing with open arms toward others acts as a summary reminder of how I hope to be as I seek to be a reconciling person in my spiritual framework and practices. In the context of my naturally intro-verted nature this is a substantial challenge.

In practice, both internally in the village and outwardly in relationships, this reconciling spiritual framework seeks to keep the dialogue going. It is a bridge building spiritual frame, one that is communal, collegial, consensual and committed to con-versation as life moves forward.

In the spirit of reconciliation, I find that this framework may well require of me sacrifice. In order to build a bridge, to connect or re-connect with others, I may need to accept restraints, bound-aries, disciplines and the setting of limits. I may need to listen with great care to a different point of view, to open myself to a new perspective on an issue or project. I may be invited to realise that my own treasured point of view is limited and sometimes not adequate to the matter at hand.

It is true that there are many things I do not understand or know. I have found it a great relief to admit and honour this truth in my life. Reconciliation invites me to acknowledge my limits. In the spirit of reconciliation, I am challenged to remember that life is not simply about me; life is about us. Recently in my journal reflections I wrote, "There is no them, there is only us." I have also created another collage poster with these words to deepen my sense of this truth.

Here again is the ongoing dance between self and other, the individual and the community. Here is the ever-present challenge to build the bridge, extend the welcome, listen with care, reach out with respect make sacrifice and sometimes choose the "other" over our own self-interest or desire. In my experience the path of reconciliation has often been the more challenging path to choose and follow, yet it is the path that has often led to a greater fullness of life. Some years ago a friend remarked with a laugh that, when faced with two options in decision-making, the more challenging option is usually the better of the two.

In the inner realm of the soul, reconciliation is a pathway that is ours to choose, and with committed effort we can find a way to be reconciled to ourselves. In the outer realm of relationships this pathway may not always be open to us, and yet nonviolent living challenges us to reflect seriously, and to hope for, this possibility. Reconciliation, gathering in, hospitality, sacrifice all contribute to a spiritual framework that will support our efforts, both inner and outer, to live the process of peace making.

Inclusive

A nonviolent spiritual framework is inclusive. This intention is the companion of reconciliation. The hope here is to be as inclusive as is possible in every instance. The phrase "radical inclusivity" acts as a simple description of a nonviolent framework for living. This inclusivity has several aspects. By intention, this framework is inclusive in terms of community. Here we are again with this important aspect of our attitudes and practices. While our ideal is to be inclusive, it is inevitable that some of our ordinary community experiences cast a shadow of exclusion. Some communities may require specific skills or background knowledge to enable participation. In some situations we limit community groups by geography, talent, skill, age or gender. In other instances we exclude people of different points of view around social, political or economic issues. In many community experiences, exclusion is inevitable. It seems to me that what matters is to be aware of our exclusions in these everyday ways, and to affirm clearly that these do not question or demean the worth, dignity and value inherent in every person.

The image of the planet earth on the wall of my entry hall represents, for me, the ongoing challenge in terms of inclusion. My hope is to grow into a deeper understanding that I am one with the human family and by virtue of birth we are all worthy of dignity, respect and safety. This statement forms part of my personal principles that we will consider in the next chapter: "All humanity is my family; I was born into community." I read somewhere along the way that if we are able to reframe our various community relationships in the more personal terms of our larger family, we find it more and more difficult to take violent action against others. In this more personal frame we realise that, in large scale violent actions, we are attacking our kin, brothers, sisters, cousins. When we extend this to include the planet earth, we are confronted in with the truth that to savage the earth, or to treat carelessly any aspect of creation out of self-interest, we are doing violence to our home, our only home, and harming ourselves by extension. The notion of inclusive community has significant implications for living out the processes that lead to peace day by day.

Years ago, when we worked together presenting programs in the United States to assist people learning about the role of spiritual directors, my then colleague, Alan W. Jones, summarised the sense of human community in our faith tradition in this simple and blunt assertion. He said, "What it means is that you are stuck with me and I am stuck with you." So it is; we do not choose those with whom we share life on this planet, we are all in this together. Such an inclusive framework challenges us to begin with this vision of our being one, even when in instances we set limits to a smaller community gathering for local and specific purposes.

What is true of my life in these outer realms, is also true of my life in the village of my soul. A nonviolent spiritual framework works to include everyone who appears in the village, the inner community. Here again is radical inclusivity, and our intention to be diligent and disciplined in this exercise directly affects our success in being open to the fact of our sharing life together as one – the human family. An important principle that has supported our work in the Nonviolence and Interfaith Leadership Program is that inner leads to outer. It is true for me that what I will not engage within I will project onto others. My rejection of others tells me a great deal about the issues I am avoiding in my own soul. I am reminded again that I can learn a lot about myself by noticing those who I tend to keep as my enemies in one form or another. I often reflect on how autobiographical are my judgements and criticisms of others.

A young man once was faced with the challenge to acknowledge his rage and to incorporate that energy in image form within his inner village. We talked about an approach to the one he identified as rage, and it became clear that he was itching for a fight to put him in his place, if not eliminate him altogether. I offered the approach that rage, was actually a wounded and hurt part of his own soul. Rage represented his response to the hurts and wounds of his inner life, often caused by virtue of outer circumstances. As we talked I invited him to look upon this one in the same way he would a young man he found alone in a room crying and wounded. Would he abuse and even kick him or would he try to offer him some understanding and comfort? He chose the latter and realised that he needed to approach his own rage in the same way. I affirmed that to attack any part of us that is troublesome for any reason is to risk igniting or continuing a long-term civil war in the soul. He was able to see the truth of this for himself and he resolved to go to the rage person in his village and see what the two of them could work out together. This inner work may well lead him to outer ways of compassion in being with others.

A statement that expresses this for me focuses on compassion: "If I will embrace the suffering me, I may be able to embrace the suffering you." I have made yet another poster with this reflection. One of the most challenging and liberating encounters that I experienced early on in my own active imagination with the villagers was with a man named Anger. It took a while for us to forge a safe and respectful ground, but we did it. Later on his name then changed to Passion and I realised that hidden in the complex energies of anger and rage is an energy that is concerned deeply for my survival, well-being and dignity. I suggest that this is true for us and that this energy that is passionate about our survival and the quality of our lives cannot be released until we face the negative and destructive aspects of our angers and passions. It is a complex energy and one that enriches our lives greatly when engaged with respect and honour. The young man trying to decide how to engage his rage made a decision that will enable him to explore and understand more deeply his rage, and within this complex energy he may find the energy that seeks to help him live a creative and nonviolent life. What is true here with rage can be true of any emotion or energy, or person in the village. The transformative process is one of compassion and welcome. Nonviolent living outwardly depends on our being willing first to welcome, and include in our inner community, any who emerge along the soul's journey.

Some years ago I read Patrick White's self-portrait, *Flaws in the Glass*. Toward the end I encountered this simple sentence: "Only love redeems." It is such a simple summary statement of the entire transformative process. I took this three-word assertion into my reflections for quite a while. Subsequently I used this simple statement as a title for an entire art exhibition. In this context here, it functions as sort of a bottom line to affirm the truth that we can only experience transformation, and the growth of nonviolent living, when we approach our complex and amazing, maddening, mysterious selves with love and compassion. We are challenged to include all of who we are in our sense of self and embrace our complex selves with love.

All in

To continue with this inclusive framework, I attempt to hold together, with respect, the full range of my life's experiences. My framework challenges me to be open both to the scientific and the mythic, the rational, the non-rational and the irrational. Part of me is given to thoughtful, rational reflection, and an academic orientation to life. Part of me also is at home in the realm of the mystical: synchronistic experiences, meaningful coincidences with no apparent causal connection, and the deeper, symbolic dimension of simple, literal events in life. Another part of me, somewhat irrational, is capable of jumping quickly to the catastrophic, over-dramatising an experience and expecting the worst. During my wife's last illness, I found a book on her bookshelf that intrigued me. I began to read it and found it of enormous help in those present circumstances. At one point I asked her where it had come from and she smiled and told me I had purchased it about a year earlier. I had no recollection of this, and was even more amazed that my eyes fell on it during this challenging time. I have had more than one friend comment on the experience of seeing a book on a bookstore shelf that seemed to jump out at them. From the point of view of synchronicity, the book was just the right book to read for that time. Within the last year I again turned to my own bookshelves to find a book to take with me to hospital for my scheduled open-heart surgery. I chose to re-read one that I had first read almost twenty years earlier. It turned out again to be a remarkable choice. When I was able after surgery to concentrate enough to read, the reflections in the book spoke deeply to my own circumstance. These experiences invite us to reflect with care on the meaning of so called random events. Our challenge is to include the mythic and symbolic dimensions of our experiences as being meaningful to our life experiences.

For me, the dream as a symbolic story is a relevant example of the non-rational, mythic experience that can be used as a resource to guide us as we seek to live a nonviolent life. As I understand it, the scientific community affirms that we dream three to five times each night. To engage the images of these stories symbolically and with careful reflection, can result in ongoing guidance, wisdom, and insights for daily living. There is much written about the dream experience flowing on from Jung's work, and I won't duplicate this. What is essential for me to affirm is the symbolic capacity of most dreams. The stories as symbolic events open me up to a rich internal landscape, one that has been a vital resource for now sixty years.

Dreams vary in function. Some come to confirm pathways taken, others warn of unwise decisions and directions, some nightmarishly so. Other dreams come to balance a lopsided, conscious point of view, to encourage a new endeavour, to close a door on a life event, or offer resolve to an old dilemma. Some dreams set a life theme before us. In my last semester at university in 1963, at age twenty-one, I had a dream that helped me identify a life theme. It was a grand dream taking place on the university campus, with a Wagnerian-like opera being performed in the area in front of the library. It was complete with underground tunnels leading from the library to other parts of the campus. The primary theme in the dream had to do with the balancing of thinking and feeling ways leading to decisions and judgements. It is a theme that continues with me in my daily living.

Another life dream emerged at age thirty-five. I woke in an agitated state from a dream in which I had visited a doctor with my wife because I was feeling unwell. The doctor told me that I had an infection in my testicles and that he would have to castrate me. I objected (as you do) so he told me I had one year in which to try to address the situation. If I could not clear up the infection he would proceed with the surgery. I shared the dream with my wife in the morning and she encouraged me to make contact with a Jungian Analyst we knew who worked nearby. This is Weyler Greene who I mentioned earlier. That day I made an appointment to seek his counsel and remained in this analytical relationship for five years. The dream challenged me to realise that my capacity to generate life for myself and others, my creative energy and its expression were in danger. Things needed to change; this signalled a life changing movement from youth to middle age, and challenged me to get serious about my creativity on many levels of life. It also was a challenge to focus regularly on the balance between caring for myself and caring for others. When I first began composing the reflections in this chapter, in July, 2016,

I had been reflecting on two dreams that made clarifying and supportive comments on the stage of my life at that time. Having experienced open-heart surgery eight months earlier, my life had changed significantly and I entered a new phase of activity and a new search for meaning. Once again daily life patterns and my sense of myself were shifting significantly, and the dreams offered support and encouragement as I made my way forward.

If I am asked to identify one single experience that has enriched my life with meaning, purpose and healing it is the gift of the dreams. Dreams have been my faithful companion and have engaged me in dialogue over these past six decades. We come again to the value and importance of inner dialogue. Out of this ongoing, dialogic relationship of following the dream trail, I am deeply enriched and supported in being at home with the mysterious complexity of myself. This all contributes substantially to a living framework that supports nonviolent living. Yes, the stories are symbolic and require effort to understand. Yes, it is time consuming to explore the significance of the symbols and movements in the narratives. Yes, it is all sometimes confusing and frustrating. Yes, the activity is counter-cultural to our dominant extraverted culture. And yes, it is also worth enduring the efforts and frustrations to gain the benefit of a deeper presence guiding, shaping, and enriching my conscious life. My life ultimately remains something of a mystery, but one that is rich with meaning and purpose. The dream also serves to underscore the truth that the wisdom I need for living well comes from within me. However much I value the input and contributions of others, life's greatest insights will emerge from within over time, and in a timely manner, and build a strong identity from within. The task is simply to surrender to the work of attending to these visitations as best I can.

Dialogue is the dynamic of the dream relationship. My dreams and my consciousness are in ongoing conversation. The dream is a "voice" that speaks, that addresses consciousness. My consciousness shares in this dialogue by attending upon the dream symbols, relating to them, de-coding them, and taking whatever action is suggested or required. All this sends a positive message of response to the dream spirit that I am attentive to the experience and welcome and value the stories that come to me.

Dream work is a deeply enriching way to engage the symbolic, mythic dimension of our lives. It is a lifelong challenge to do the work, and a lifelong privilege to be in dialogue with a wisdom voice from within. It is a significant way in which we bridge the scientific and mythic dimensions of our lives and I consider this challenge to be one of the most exciting in our present times.

An inclusive spiritual framework also will attend to both the traditional and the innovative experiences of life. I see myself as deeply grounded in a faith tradition and honour the history of my People. I am also, along with present generations, ever on the cutting edge of uncharted territory, the future. It seems true that every generation must find new words and thought patterns to express ancient truths. A friend once described this as having a kind of double vision. We honour, we treasure, the past that supports our sense of being grounded in the present, and we attend as well to the future and seek to be open to what new insights and understandings may emerge. We honour the ancients and all they offer us. Personally, I am coming to realise more and more in these elder years that I am well advised to honour and know my individual past, my shared history, both of faith and culture, and to accept how these strands come together to inform, enrich and also limit me as continue to create my ever-new future.

My inclusive spiritual framework must also make room for

changing roles and an ever-changing sense of identity as life continues to unfold. My different stages of life have invited me to shift and reconfigure my self-understanding, to include new ways of being with myself and with others. I now live in my mid-seventies, and have had serious cardiac surgery; I live with cardiac disease. I have also had a total hip replacement. I am also a widower, now a single man looking after my own home and world. I am still a father and a grandfather whose roles, in the absence of my wife, has taken on new dimensions of importance for my family and me. At times I seem to be the same man as I was in my twenties, and at others I struggle to imagine who I was then. I am still "me" to myself, yet now engage the world around me very differently. Continuity and change seem to go hand in hand. My framework includes who I was and who I am now am.

Many years ago a woman came to converse with me about the changes she faced as her children grew into adulthood. She was not needed as mother in the many ways she had functioned for years. She did not wish to cease being a mother, but needed a new direction for her energies and focus. Out of our conversations she experienced the following meditation. In the story a Queen Mother was retiring from her active role in the castle life and realm. A grand banquet was held at which she was feted for her contributions over the many years. After this there was a service of blessing, and then there was a solemn procession from the throne room to an apartment of rooms at the back of the castle where the retired Queen Mother would now live. It was a lovely, peaceful space with beautiful views through the windows. Still in the castle compound, but away from the daily business, she would be content there. The throne was now empty and it remained to be seen who now would take up that role. Some months later the woman whose story this was, took up a new direction in a field of great interest.

To reflect on the assertion that we include consciously all of life's experiences extends to the more difficult parts of the story. One year on the occasion of my birthday, a young friend took me out to dinner. During our conversation he asked me if I had any regrets. It was difficult to restrain my impulse to laugh out loud. Of course I have regrets and plenty of them. He shared a saying that was something like, "It is better to regret what we have done, than to regret what we have not done." However we say it, my lived experience affirms that we have regrets as life goes along.

As well as all the positive aspects of my history, a framework that will support nonviolent living must include those many times when I have fallen short of my own hopes, best intentions and my ideal self. My story contains many wonderful moments, achievements and successes. My story also contains failings and times of pain and injury, various forms of violence that I have inflicted, first on myself, and then on others as well. It is all here, my shadowland; this is the name I give it. I can remove nothing from my story without diminishing myself or misrepresenting myself to myself as well as to others. To include the regrets of life is to hold onto the shadow moments as an integral part of my story.

What emerges here is the truth that these shadow experiences of action, attitudes and words are often my most reliable teachers. I am reminded by them to remember who I am as an ordinary, complex, contradictory person. As a teenager I remember being told by a priest that we learn more in the valleys of life than on the mountaintops. The experiences that humiliate often encourage a deep humility in us and this can foster the compassion toward ourselves that becomes that ongoing resource of compassion for others. I remember such an event from my childhood. I would have been eight or nine. I was angry with another boy and destroyed something that he valued. It was deliberate and mean spirited. I paid the consequences as was only right, but more importantly, I still remember this incident as it reminds me of one of the aspects of my shadow side. I do have a mean streak, and I am well advised to remember this truth.

A common form of advice in the face of difficulty or wounding is to "let it go," and to "move on." Sometimes it takes the form of dismissal as "never mind." I find these troublesome sayings; they represent an approach that, for me, does not seem to work. The danger is that we will simply bury those more difficult times and experiences, and they will quietly fester and feed the civil war within. My experience teaches me that I must engage fully the experiences I regret and ask what they teach me about myself. Who are these parts of me, the villagers, who hold to harsh judgements because of differences? Who is this one who acts in wilful self-interest regardless of the cost to others? Who is the one who dismisses or overrides other peoples' points of view? These can be difficult reflections that sometimes lead to deep sadness, frustration and regret. In this regard, I hold to the truth that such sombre moments of regret often lubricate the soul and prevent us from becoming dry, hard and brittle people.

In the long term picture of my life I can see that there have been times when I could not come to grips with myself consciously except through an experience I later viewed with regret. These are the valleys of regret, these are the experiences that grounded me in the ordinary nature of my life, these are the painful times that serve to help me be more honest with the shadow side, and that lubricated the soul. I have not let go, moved on or dismissed them; they have remained with me as great teachers. When I was a teenager, another priest once counselled me that "suffering equals maturity." I can't argue with this truth though I would still like to. My mother used to say when noting someone's unfortunate behaviour, "There but for the grace of God go I." This, too, carries a truth that I can't escape. If humans can do it, I can do it. At times the shadow parts of me who live within the soul, the village, can be very challenging to my ideal self. Compassion for my own complex, contradictory humanity enables me to embrace others who also struggle with life in regretful ways. Inner leads to outer; it is all here, right here.

Both-and ... either/or

In considering the character of a framework that is inclusive and that will support nonviolent living, I have affirmed the importance of both-and thinking. We usually position this against either/or thinking, and to a significant degree this is true for me. This being stated, I also realise that there are times when the either/or approach to a situation, or attitude, is also of importance. In the Christian Gospel of St. Matthew these words are attributed to Jesus. "No one can serve two masters; for a slave will either hate the one and love the other, or be devoted to the one and despise the other. You cannot serve God and wealth" (Matthew 6:24, RSV translation). I do not want to get side tracked into an exploration of the word translated "wealth," sometimes "mammon." The issue here for me is that I cannot have more than one number One. At the core of my being there is only room for one primary concern. Paul Tillich asserted that our God is our Ultimate Concern, regardless of our conscious creedal allegiances. Whatever is our ultimate concern shapes the entire nature of our lives. There is enough truth here to be annoying and useful. I am pushed to ask myself what is my one number One. What is my ultimate concern? This is an either/or way of thinking that, for me, is crucial. Recently I have been asking myself what one word I would choose as the benchmark and measure of my entire life. If I have to choose one word to define and shape the character of my living, what will it be? No easy task; I am still working on it. There are those moments or times when the either/or equation is essential. They may be few, but they are critical. One experience challenged me to the core over forty-five years ago when I realised I have an addictive personality, and that I was addicted to alcohol. I realised I had to choose sobriety or face the consequences of alcoholism. There was no middle ground, no blending of opposites, no this and that. It was clearly either/or and I knew it to be a lifelong decision. There was no going back. With many tears and in great fear I chose sobriety, and am still grateful. Complete abstention was my only life giving option. "Either/or" was the critical ground for my choosing. Over fifty years ago it was also true of smoking. This, too, was an either/or decision. I had tried cutting down and quitting temporarily, and nothing worked. I finally gave in and quit; either/or was the best possible path for the decision.

Having now honoured these few, but critical, moments, I recognise that an inclusive framework for nonviolent living involves a commitment to both-and living most of the time. This commitment allows us to engage the ordinary complexities of life, and to affirm that, in many instances, in matters of the soul and in relationships, two things, or more, can be true at once. As I mentioned, I grew up in a worldview that valued highly simple, clear-headed and straightforward thinking and confident decision-making. Knowing one's own mind, being consistent in one's opinions and being decisive without hesitation were considered signs of maturity. I have come over the years to see things very differently. With the community of inner villagers in mind, in the light of the complexities of my outside life and relationships, I am more inclined to see that ambivalence may be a sign of the engaged and mature mind. I return to the language tool, "part of me." Part of me sees things one way, and part of me sees things another way. I do not always agree with myself, and this is stating the situation mildly. Sometimes I am simply dumbfounded by the differences on which I touched briefly a bit earlier. Engaging difference and conflict creatively, both within and with others, has become an important tool for living.

Two things

A natural flow on from both-and thinking is the truth that two things can be true at once. Indeed, two things, or more, can be true at once. I remember well the day after I chose sobriety. I was resting on the bed calculating that, if I lived to be eighty-one, I would have to live fifty years without a drink! This is one reason people in AA practice the principle of living one day at a time! For me there was terror in those quiet reflections, and also a deep sense of relief. I had known for at least ten years that alcohol and I did not get along, and finally I had taken action to liberate myself from its tyranny. Over the early weeks, while I occasionally had hand tremors, I also had a deep sense of peace, freedom and an astonishing surge of energy. Two things can be true at once, both-and living characterises the nonviolent way, the pathway of peace.

Perhaps the most painful occasion of this experience came when my wife died in 2009. She had lived with cancer for only eight months. Those months were, in many ways, a remarkable time of closeness and sharing, though it was also painful and haunted by the reality of death. When she finally died I was shattered, exhausted, numb at times and certainly unsure of what life meant for me now. Also, I was relieved and at peace. My children and I gave her a good death. There was an indescribable peace and serenity in all that transpired and I knew it to be grace-filled. Two things can be true at once. It was a serene and devastating time. In this way of living we include the complexities of our lives, which are with us daily in small as well as in grand ways. If life is to be rich, whole, and our way of living is to sustain nonviolence inner and outer, then both-and thinking will, most often, be the path that makes this possible.

Two things can be true at once. This affirmation provides us with a way of dealing with the complexities we experience in ourselves and that we observe and encounter in others. This is a particularly useful perspective when we encounter the shadow, both in ourselves and in our dealings with others. If I am to be inclusive in my framework for creating peace building and supporting nonviolent living, then I must make room for the fact that I sometimes act out of my shadow and make comments or take actions that are hurtful, demeaning, dismissive or abusive of others. I do try to acknowledge shadow energies in my journal writing and quiet reflections, and then discipline my words and actions, yet sometimes I express shadow material toward others without much thought. It fascinates me that we are often surprised at the shadow sides of public figures when the public media brings this to our attention. If we understand the shadow side of ourselves, how can we be surprised when it is manifest in others? I have long concluded that acknowledging, engaging and including the shadow in our self-understanding is perhaps the most important and difficult aspect of developing a framework to support my desire to live nonviolently. The hero and villain are right here. Until we face up to this, the internal civil war goes on unchecked.

Both-and thinking, two things can be true at once, acknowledging the shadow, these perspectives are all the ground work for developing a framework for making peace and living nonviolently.

Compassion

If being inclusive is the core of the nonviolent life, compassion is the manner in which this inclusive intention is expressed. The etymology of the word includes the willingness to suffer with, and for me this includes suffering with myself so that I may be open to suffering with others. The two are tightly bound together. Again, the degree to which I am able to engage myself with compassion, to suffer even the most discomforting aspects of me, governs the degree to which I am able to provide a compassionate response to the lives of others.

There are two other aspects of the notion of compassion that are important for us. First, compassion involves sacrifice. In order to cultivate compassion toward myself, I need to sacrifice the certainty of my ego conscious point of view and to be open to alternate ways of looking at life. This then flows on to how I am with others. Compassion for others, being able to connect with them, to have empathy for their pain, or to take interest in their lives, requires that I turn my gaze toward others and sacrifice my preoccupation with my own needs. Here again the eternal dance of self-other comes into play. In moments of compassion I make the effort to put others first and set aside my self-concerned way of being in the world. While the language around sacrifice may seem a little remote, I conclude that the experiences of sacrifice, even daily, are not. Anyone engaged in an enduring relationship will know this, regardless of the terms used to describe the experience.

Second, I read somewhere over the years that the root of the word compassion is connected to the word "womb," which offers an understanding of compassion as an act of deep maternal caring, bonding and of nurture, that can be enacted both by women and men. This womb-like caring also asks of us sacrifice as any mother can attest.

Compassion refers not only an attitude or point of view, it also gives form and shape to the character of our actions. Marcus Borg, in his writing, *The Heart of Christianity*, asserts that this is a core characteristic shared by all the major world faith traditions. The Dalai Lama, in the *Book of Joy* makes the same claim. This being the case, I consider it safe to assert that compassion is the core ethical expression of the major faith traditions. It is the way we are meant to be with each other. It is an essential aspect of nonviolent living and the making of peace. Compassion here goes beyond acts of charity. Compassion is a requirement laid on the souls of all humanity in our interactions with each other. It is a radical demand.

The nature of compassion is radically inclusive. It is the open arms of hospitality, gathering others into our worlds and lives. It is caring, but mutual caring for each other according to needs, and it is both just and merciful. Compassion challenges us to sustain our commitments to human solidarity, human equality, human dignity and the common good for all.

However, sweeping and grand statements may leave us with no sense of how to respond, except with some sense that we have failed. I have come to understand over time that I am meant to express my compassion in the context of my given life, and this is most often in the form of "small gestures." Within the limits of my life there are many opportunities daily to be an inclusive, hospitable person. Occasions abound in which I am able to embody hospitality, to give it flesh. Loneliness is widespread in my culture. I can act in small ways to connect with people in the ordinary flow of life. Regular walks are now a routine part of my days since my open-heart surgery. On these walks I have set the intention to greet those I encounter along the way. I am motivated by a desire to refuse to be part of the alienation that seems rife in my suburban life, and to affirm our human solidarity, even if only in a brief greeting and smile. Sometimes I get back a grunt, many other times a smile and a return greeting, and at other times a full on conversation opens up about the day, the garden, the states of our health, our exercises, even stories about family members. Sometimes the other person initiates the greeting and rarely am I ignored. I add, by the way, that I do not call out to someone facing away from me who is on a ladder! Likewise at the swimming pool where I exercise, I make the attempt to greet my colleagues in the walking lane where the humorous return to "How are you?" is sometimes that "I am vertical, breathing and above ground!" I am surprised at the stories that sometimes pour out, and the bits and pieces of life that we share.

Stories abound. I remember with fondness the small, older Irish woman with whom I walked for four blocks one morning. She gave me a non-stop commentary on contemporary life lamenting the lack of connections and neighbourliness among us. I barely got a word in, agreed with much of what I heard, and got a blessing as we parted. What a woman! At the shopping mall one morning I saw a woman coming up the ramp toward me.

She was very stooped over, and her face and movement told me clearly that walking was an effort. Slung across her body was a wonderfully coloured purse, so I took the opportunity to comment on the colourful beauty of her handbag. Her face lit up like the proverbial Christmas tree, as she thanked me. It was just a moment … and it was a moment. The man walking his little dog paused and we began to talk. Issues of international concern soon became our focus. He, too, is a migrant, and we exchanged phone numbers in order to set a time for a cuppa to talk more. Who knows where things will go? I complimented a man on his garden as he was watering in some newly set in plants I had not seen before. Out poured a background on the plants and an invitation to see the lush tropical garden along the front entrance of his unit. It was very impressive and he offered to show me the back garden next time I came by. That may yet happen. These are small gestures, making connections, breaking through loneliness, putting flesh on compassion. There is much I can no longer do, but these things I can do, and the ethical imperative is upon me to act. It has taken me so many years to realise how important it is to leave the house with intention, not just to shop or do an errand, but to be a person of hospitality, connection, interested in others, and ready to extend the gathering arms in small gestures of compassion. My tradition teaches me that if I am faithful in small matters, I may be able to be faithful in greater ones when the need arises. Small gestures of compassion add a positive spirit to the collective well being of us all. For me, it has become critical to engage this imperative with serious intent to break though the tragic alienation of contemporary life and to sustain nonviolent living.

Creation

Finally, a framework that will support nonviolent living and build peaceful pathways among us includes for me a growing sense of my oneness with, and my participation in, the entire creation. It sounds somewhat grand, actually a bit overwhelming, but I am learning that the dialogue with creation I mentioned earlier is critical to my well-being, and to our well-being as a planetary family. Our current concerns about climate change have served to make this even more clear. It interests me greatly, even excites me, after decades of framing myself in a psychological frame, to consider reframing my life in a larger ecological point of view as a participant in the world soul as Hillman names it. I find it an exciting challenge to consider what it actually means for us to move from being anthropocentric to biocentric in our understanding of ourselves in the midst of the creation.

An article by a New York writer, Tyler Caine, introduced me to the term "biophilia." He credits E. O. Wilson for bringing the term into the larger scientific discourse in 1980. Biophilia affirms that we humans have an inborn emotional affiliation with all other living organisms. Caine asserts that we are indeed hardwired to love nature. It interests me to note how often people speak of turning to a park, the ocean, a river, a mountain, the bush, the desert, a garden, flowers, trees and other experiences of nature for refreshment, renewal and healing. It has certainly been true of me with my walks along the shore years ago in the midst of an unexpected depression, and even now with times of sitting in the garden among the vegetables and native plants, focusing on the potted plants or listening to the birds in the early morning. Reframing our self-understandings in regard to the creation has become an urgent matter in the face of the ever expanding concern for the health of the planet and our natural resources, and the changes in our global climate. The tree on my front verge and I are in an ongoing and important relationship in terms of planetary health. I am no longer apart from nature, but a part of nature, indeed in the midst, and my nonviolent approach to life, overall, must include my deep regard, respect of, and love for, the natural world which is my home, our home. In my reflections I am intent on being a part of being, and no longer the master of being. Gandhi's simple principle "All is one" continues to place the challenge before us all.

Along with this is an ongoing concern for the just distribution of the planet's resources and our produced goods. In the face of our oneness as a human family, and our shared places with creation on the planet, nonviolent living challenges us to see to it that the dignity of each human being is considered, affirmed, and honoured as we live together on our global home. We are a long way from this, and the just distribution of goods and resources is a growing and substantial challenge to us as we understand how to live with each other with care and respect, and as members of one family, one creation. We cannot go on living in western culture as we have done for far too long. Our planet home cannot endure the strain of providing for us as we have demanded. We have been violent, abusive and insensitive to our planetary home. The near future will demand much of us if we are all to be afforded the respect, opportunities and care that we all deserve. I suppose for me it is important to see this not as deprivation, but as opportunity and adventure. It will matter greatly what mindset we choose for ourselves as we move forward. Gandhi's three words both haunt us and inspire us forward in developing a nonviolent framework for living: "All is one."

This section of these reflections has a feeling of a whirlwind tour. We have considered three qualities that obstruct the cultivation of a nonviolent framework: purity, perfection and dualism. We have then covered much terrain in the landscape of the soul as we have considered key characteristics that will support our efforts to create peace and live nonviolently. These include the overall dynamic of reconciliation, the intention to be inclusive in terms of our inner communities, and in our overall interactions with others. We have also considered the importance of both-and and either/or thinking, the shadow (again!), compassion and our relationship to the entire creation. Making the time to consider these consciously can indeed feel a bit overwhelming, and yet it can also liberate us to live with a greater confidence and intention, a life that supports nonviolence and then shares the benefits of this work with others. In the next section we will give consideration to some ways that help us strengthen our intentions with supportive practices.

CHAPTER FIVE

Exploring Tools to Help Us

In the previous four chapters we have considered our sense of place and our heritage that travels with us, we have reflected on the experience of community, both inner and outer, and reflected on the importance of dialogue in our nonviolent spiritual framework. We have also engaged the mysterious Other in Jung's notion of the shadow, personal, collective and golden. Our reflections have included matters that affect our framework, and characteristics that are essential to our framework for nonviolent living.

We come now to our final chapter in which we think about some tools to help us sustain this framework. I often think of this as the "how to" part of these reflections. How do we ground these reflections in particular and everyday practices? How do these insights, affirmations and assertions influence the rhythm of our living?

My reflections here are around three specific matters that give grounding, how to, to our framework. I intend to reflect on self-care, personal principles and ways to engage the shadow. The faith traditions of the world's major religions offer many individual, rich and varied guidelines for practices that will help sustain a spiritual framework. Our communities abound with timeless insights of great value. The task for each of us, within our own context, is to explore, and experiment with, what is on offer. The mix of rhythms and practices will vary for us depending on our individual character and our community context, and in all likelihood these rhythms and patterns will shift and change for us over time as we move along in life.

Self care

Whenever I stop to consider the matter of self-care, I am amazed to realise again how we have made such hard work of something so obvious and so important, yet it seems we have done so. I know that, certainly, I have done so. More often than not, when someone comes to consult with me, one of the major issues that soon emerges is this matter of self-care. For many, taking care of oneself seems to be connected with weakness. For others, this issue betrays a subtle sense of being unworthy of care and concern, and yet for others it is contrary to a particular spiritual teaching that places others before us. I remember a young man who grew up in a somewhat conservative faith tradition telling me that he was trained to put himself last. "JOY" was the key word: Jesus first, others second, and you last. He found it difficult at first to engage self care with any comfort. Some decades ago a woman consulted me about her need to re-frame a sense of focus for her life as her children were growing up and needed less of her attention and time. I suggested that she might want to set aside a time each week to pursue an interest of her own. She was horrified at such a selfish thought and did not come to see me again. I still marvel at a commercial for a cold remedy that I saw years ago on the television that showed young business types taking a tablet and marching off to work with a briefcase in hand even though they felt unwell. The lyrics to the catchy tune included, "soldier on." Some years later this switched to a scenario of a thoughtful young man or woman staying home from work and not taking the flu to the office while the neighbour sneezed his way to the car and off to the office. Recently I have noticed that the thoughtful ones are gone and we are again encouraged to "soldier on." This is a fascinating advertising commercial making comment on culture, or perhaps shaping culture. I am also pleased to hear growing, dissenting voices that tell people to stay at home when unwell.

Responsible self-care is essential to cultivate peace and to sustain a nonviolent way of living, a nonviolent spirituality. In this instance we are now considering explicitly the nature of an embodied, nonviolent spiritual framework for living. If I am violent to myself, how can I possibly offer you care, consideration and compassion? Many years ago a colleague and I were talking about our work. She summarised the need to look after herself with this one line that I have quoted more times than I can remember: "If I feel deprived, everyone will suffer." The degree to which I look after myself – body, soul, mind and spirit – will directly affect the degree to which I will be able to support anyone else in the same endeavour. Also years ago, when my children were young, I commented to a man over the phone that I had too many meetings on and was out every night of a week. His comment in return was to "join the club" like the rest. He could offer no support as his life also was under a similar pressure, and he was not looking after himself or his family relationships. If I do not look after me, I can't assist you in looking after you.

In a sense woven into the fabric of self-care is a strong thread of an ethical imperative. It is a vital act of social justice. In my culture, the mental health resources are continually strained. The pressure arises from people who are driven to achieve dreams of success or service that are often unrealistic. These are often dreams and ideals set from the outside by culture, family and even faith traditions. It is long been my conviction that we, in western, consumer driven societies, have created an inhumane culture that is soulless in its core concerns. In this environment it takes great courage, even heroic effort, to define our individual self-care program and to enact such a life rhythm. There is another poem by Meister Eckhart, translated by Daniel Ladinsky in *Love Poems from God*. This poem speaks of an insidious idol that creates ongoing conflict within people around needs and desires. The idol is commerce. The poem asserts that commerce has become a god, a weapon, an idol, "in the hands of the insane." Eckhart lived in the 13th and 14th centuries. It seems we have long been encouraged to strive after ideals that others shape for us.

To begin to develop a life-affirming program of self-care, this question is a helpful starting place: What must I do to be well? The "must" here is essential in that it represents the ethical imperative both for me and for my culture. If I am not well, I will then offer the world around me my unwell self, who is quite likely to resent or criticise others for my own failings. What must I do to be well?

Self-care takes us to the simple daily ground of our lives. How much sleep do I need to feel rested? What about my diet? Am I taking appropriate exercise? How is my work-leisure balance? Do I feel well connected to others both intimately, and socially? Do I carve out time alone for reflection, reading and quiet, as well a time for participation in social and group events? What am I doing for entertainment and relaxation? Who are those in my life I value, whose opinions are important to me, who help me shape my life, and assist me in my being well? Whose counsel do I seek when I am unsure about how to proceed in life?

The questions that prod us along can take many forms. Each of us can design our own, or reflect with a trusted friend to focus on our personal concerns and issues. We each need also to identify the present context in which we seek to be well, and to recognise that the context itself may need to change to support our efforts at wellness. We each need to bring into consciousness the social justice aspect of self-care, and the ethical imperative that comes from this recognition.

Self-care is, as we say, not rocket science. Ordinary illustrations from my conversations with others are wonderful examples. One man returned to an old love from his youth and took up woodworking. Over time this took shape into working with non-electrical tools and becoming himself the engine that created the product. In our conversations he came to see this as an integral part of his spiritual practice. It involves the alchemical process of turning a rough piece of wood with minimal value into something of beauty and usefulness, and contributes to his well-being. He has also been able to join with another and offer workshops for others who seek the simple quiet process of this form of creative activity. In our conversations I came to see more clearly that this speaks to my fascination with collage as a form of art creation. Taking scraps of papers and creating images of colour and form touches deeply into my soul and contributes to the sense of grounded wellness that I can then share with others. Sitting at the table in my studio is a sacred place and time.

Years ago I watched another colleague give up his 5:00pm, after work, glass of sherry and, return to the piano for thirty minutes each afternoon instead. It had been years since he had touched it, and the impact on him was a softening of his presentation of himself to the rest of us. It clearly was a soulful encounter for him. Another man, in the midst of stress from overwork in a demanding position, returned to playing his guitar daily and eventually ended up forming a band of friends just like in his youth. He was pleased to report that, in addition to playing for their own enjoyment, they even got a gig now and then. Some of us take up regular meditation, yoga or jogging, others get on the bike, or go to the pool for exercise and a swim. Some find wellness sustained by cleaning the house. I find it in doing the laundry each week and keeping things up to date. Some sit down, rest and read a book with a cup of coffee or tea, others get up and get active, perhaps out in the garden or by taking a walk. A colleague told a group of us of a friend who debriefed herself on the way home from work each day, and if she arrived at her driveway still with things to consider, she drove around the block until she could let go of work and enter her home focussed on family. For some it may be the kindly act of enjoying a bubble bath or a leisurely morning sleep in. Yet for others it could be the pleasure of having a day out in the park, on a hiking trail, or going to a movie. For some it will involve serious reflection on the present context of work. There are times when re-framing our working pattern, or looking for a new job, may well be a substantial and necessary act of self-care.

The examples are endless. The challenge is specific to each of us. Recently I talked with a colleague about weight and weight loss. We both agreed that the charts of the norms were of little use for us. This is true of many charts and systems or practices of self-care that are available in our culture. Each of us has to work it out for ourselves, and comparisons with norms and other people, including good friends, may distract us rather than offer us our solutions. The most trusted and vital source of wisdom in these matters resides within us. Yes, it is important to talk things out with that trusted person, but then we decide and we act from within. It is a process of informed discernment, and the discernment changes as the circumstances of daily life changes.

In this tapestry of self-care, there are several other threads on which I want to reflect briefly. One is the puzzling attitude of many toward medication. So often I hear people speak about their necessary medications with a sense of resentment or of failure. Perhaps this is due to some false understanding in our western culture of independence and the virtue of being strong. In an age wherein we are blessed with many scientific and medical tools to help us be well, it seems a strange response to view the taking of medications as somehow an unfortunate circumstance. I do not align with this attitude. I am grateful to live in a time when medications are available to assist us in being well. For me, they do not excuse me from my personal work of reflection and self-understanding, rather they make it more possible. In some instances these medications may make significant contributions to our well-being and our capacity to enact a nonviolent way of living. While medications need to be monitored carefully to prevent inappropriate use or undesirable side effects, I have come to approach my tablets with a sense of gratitude. It seems that, presently, I cannot be well and safe without them. I was deeply impressed in my teens on hearing a woman compare taking necessary medications with taking the sacramental elements in the Christian Eucharist. She maintained that the development of such medications is due to the divine wisdom that drives the souls of many to work for our betterment. Her story reminds me to be grateful as well as discerning in using medications.

This sense of being strong and independent flows over to the notion of life with limits. In a culture that seems to revere the young, vital, athletic and strong, how do I acknowledge and accept with dignity my limits as I continue to age? A time came some years back when self-care (and my wife) dictated that I no longer climb the ladder and onto the roof of the house. Limits actually came early for me when my birth related back condition was diagnosed at twenty-two. I was called off the tennis court and also told never to jog or run. I admit that pain was a helpful contributor to be accepting of these limits and the mind numbing exercises that went with the care. Self-care limits required me to wear a brace for years, and I still have one handy for days when I will be standing a good deal of the time. Self-care limits have required me often to seek a place to sit whenever possible. Acceptance was a major issue. It took me about ten years to grow to an acceptance of my own body and my limits and to realise that, in this context, I can still create a life of value and meaning and make significant contributions to others.

I am hardly alone in this need to embrace my limits. Many of us wrestle with the same reality in countless different forms. Compassionate self-care invites us to step aside from the dominant cultural notions of independence and self-reliance and to look after ourselves with that compassion which we have previously considered.

Many of these aspects of self-care bring us to the hard reality that self-care is often sustained by hard work, discipline and sacrifice. There are times when it is really difficult to stay with it. Daily yoga or meditation sounds a bit romantic and liberating. These practices are also hard work, and require us sometimes to step over our resistances and get on with it. Actually this may be why self-care often falls off the back of the truck, so to speak. It is hard work. In a culture that seems to thrive on feeling good, self-care may make hard-edged demands on us in order to work toward well-being. I am committed to regular exercise in the swimming pool. More than half of the time I only get there after I give myself a good push out the door. Often our efforts at well-being may in fact not feel good in the moment, but rather result in us feeling well overall.

When I reflect on the entire matter of self-care from the vantage point of my mid-seventies, I wonder from time to time what in fact is the function of old age. We are able to live longer these days, but to what purpose? What's the point of living longer, if there is no point, purpose, or meaning in this experience?

The mid-seventies, I am told is now "young." For me, this feels like somehow avoiding the notion of "old," as if it is hopeless, helpless and meaningless. We still seem to avoid the notion of "old," or old age, as if it is somehow wrong or unfortunate. In some traditional cultures, as I understand it, often the elders were the custodians and teachers of the community culture. Their task was to ground the young in their heritage, and share with them the stories that gave life meaning and purpose. I see older people working longer, perhaps shorter hours each week, and in less demanding positions, but working. Many of us with grey hair look after grandchildren for parents who are both at work full or part time. Perhaps in these relationships the stories of our families and cultures are shared and passed along. I am not clever enough to declare answers to these interesting questions, but I do pose the question for myself. "What is the function of my elder years?" "What am I meant to be doing now?" It is a work in progress. Perhaps this is another of those questions that we live into, rather than answer finally. Certainly I find myself drawn to be a presence to my family and to share stories when appropriate. I also find it important to give advice only when asked! I also continue to work with others in limited and significant ways that offer enrichment to them and that certainly is enriching to me. This leads me to the final thread that I am drawn to consider in terms of self-care.

Self-care for me is related directly to the common good. If we take the notion of human solidarity seriously, then it seems to me such a stance calls into question any sense of a private life and private acts. Since I am at one with the human family, all that I do daily is in the context of the common good. My efforts at self-care, nonviolent living, and peacebuilding all flow on into the larger reality of the human family. What I do, I do for us. Much of my life is personal, some of it intensely so, but if I am connected to you, to you all, then the energy of my life flows naturally into the collective energy of our neighbourhoods, cultures, nations, world. In the spiritual context of the oneness of the human family, and a larger oneness with all creation, life can be deeply personal, but not private, and it is for the common good. Such a point of view invites me to consider just what energy I am putting into the shared energy and spirit of humanity as we all struggle to live lives of meaning and purpose on this planet, our island home, the pale blue dot. In the end, my self-care has a global context, and in this sense is a concern for social justice in the widest context.

Principles

During the time I am writing these reflections, I walk almost daily in my neighbourhood and pass a construction site where some men are laying in the brick wall structures of a new house. Years ago I read a reflection about a brick wall, and the stress was on the importance of getting the foundation row of bricks straight and true. If the first, the foundation, row is not laid in accurately and solidly, the entire structure will be weakened. It is the most important row of bricks. It is interesting to note that, once completed, no one sees this row of bricks. Yet the accuracy of its line and set are essential to the success of the project. It is instructive to ponder the significance of this insight: what is often of greatest importance is unseen, out of sight from daily activity and thought.

The parable attributed to Jesus in the Gospel of Matthew, chapter 7, about the foundation of the house being built on sand or rock, makes the same point. In the story context, the house built on sand is liable to collapse in tumultuous times. The house built on a rock foundation will stand firm in times of storm and stress. The foundation of our framework for living a nonviolent life is essential to our capacity to sustain this way of living. For me, principles are the bedrock. I would suggest that we each carry within us these principles, or core beliefs. The issue is to bring the matter of our principles into our conscious reflections so that we choose, with conscious intention, those principles that will guide us in our living, rather than being carried along unconsciously by the principles of our cultures, that is, family, society, and faith tradition. Without this exercise of conscious reflection, we risk holding onto essential principles that do not match our emerging understanding of life, and working from principles that we may have, in fact, outgrown.

Principles are another way of identifying our core beliefs. Together these become a personal creed of faith that shapes our attitudes and thoughts, that claims our loyalty, guides our actions, and gives vitality to our visions, hopes and dreams. This creed of principles forms a context or container for what we believe is possible in corporate human life, and individually in our personal lives. They are our bedrock, the bottom row of bricks, on which our living rests, and from which our energies and values for living will emerge.

Gandhi identified a list of principles that acted as the foundation to his work in nonviolence. I once googled his name and the word "principles," and came up with an almost endless list of sites identifying eight to twelve principles attributed to him. What matters here is the example of one who laid in the first row of bricks carefully and built on those.

For more than ten years, under the auspices of Pace e Bene Australia, colleagues and I presented programs on nonviolence and peacebuilding. These residential retreat/conferences, were first entitled, "Mainstreaming Nonviolence" and later, the "Nonviolent Interfaith Leadership Program." As our work developed and matured, and following the example of Gandhi, my co-facilitators and I decided that we, too, would identify the principles that undergird our work. We were a staff of three then, and we organised to meet for a day of reflection to work on this project. We were sure that we'd tidy it up before lunch. We began with each of us taking strips of paper on which we wrote words that were important to us. These we stuck to the wall, and then began to group them into clusters. As we worked and talked, themes began to emerge and we began to group the words around them. We then began to try to organise words into short declarative statements. By this time lunch was long past and it was getting close to time for dinner. We ended the day knowing we had more work to do! As a staff of three, we had been meeting almost weekly to build our working relationships, and it took the next two evening sessions to complete this task. We ended up with six statements that form the foundation of our work. What we had planned to accomplish in two to three hours, took well over ten hours to complete. Subsequent staff teams for our programs signed off on this list of six principles. Here is the result of our original work as an example of the first row of bricks.

1. Community
Our individuality exists within the given reality of diverse and complex communities.

2. Interconnectedness
We are integral parts of a living organism, a community without boundaries that we see as sacred, and that is continually evolving.

3. Mystery and Paradox
We see life and relationships as unfolding mysteries.

4. My Place in the Mystery
Our individual challenge is to discover our unique place in the mystery of life.

5. The Inner Life
Our inner work shapes our outer lives.

6. Life with Others
Nonviolent living is grounded in faith and hope, and is expressed in love, mercy, justice, compassion and forgiveness.

Following on from this very enlivening exercise, I decided to take up the challenge for myself and compose what would be my own principles for nonviolent living. Having done this exercise with the group, I assumed that I would churn out an acceptable list in quick time. Wrong! It took me about eight more hours to create the eight statements that now are my principles. For several years I recited these aloud twice most days. A I find recitation aloud has a way of helping me hear them more deeply. I note the interpretation of them each time is usually different and this creates attentiveness to one or two of the principles at a specific time. The oral recitation has a way of grounding me again on what is my first row of bricks, my foundation. These give shape to my beliefs, my loyalties, my ground for action and my visions for what is desirable, even possible, in seeking to live a nonviolent life.

When we did this exercise as a staff of three, we identified the six headings or themes, and the statements given then follow these. While I have omitted the stated themes, these are woven into the tapestry of my personal reflections. These include an affirmation of divinity and the oneness of life, the limits of my understanding in the face of life as mystery, the sense of vocation for my life in the context of the mystery, my understanding of community, and the assertion that inner soul work influences deeply outer interactions. In the context of my faith tradition, I name the personal experience of the way of the cross as being central to wholeness and the experience of love, I affirm the centrality of love in all human interactions, and declare my hope for justice and mercy. While I struggled at times with the exercise, because of my need to get the words just right, I have been greatly helped in clarifying those principles on which I want to stand and that I desire deeply to shape my life. The result has been well worth the effort, and I commend highly the task of naming clearly that first row of bricks that are foundational to our desire to live nonviolent lives. Here then are the eight principles that I now use for guiding my own life. They were written in May, 2010, and I changed a word in part four in May, 2020.

The change has broadened my family from "humanity" to a sense of family that includes all creation.

The divine spirit is the life energy of all that is:
all life is interconnected.

At the heart of all life is mystery:
there are many truths I do not know.

My call is to live my life in this larger spirit-life and mystery:
wholeness, not perfection, is my hope.

All creation is my family:
I was born into community.

My inner work shapes my outer life:
what I do not engage within I project onto others.

The way of the cross is the journey to wholeness:
it is the path of love.

Loving is the most important human action:
forgiving is at the core of nonviolent living.

Justpeace is my ongoing hope:
mercy tempers the passion of justice.

The recitation aloud of these principles means a great deal to me, and to hear them daily invites me to measure my days by them and the Spirit that is in them.

Engaging the Shadow

In chapter two we focussed entirely on the shadow in three ways, the personal, the collective and the golden shadow. The agenda here now is how to do shadow work. Once we acknowledge the presence of shadow energy, what do we do with it? As we attend to this important task, I want to begin by affirming again that the shadow is a natural part of our psychic life, the unlived life or the Other. The shadow includes parts of us who complement our chosen conscious perspective. The shadow is not a problem to fix, nor is it a task to do once for all. Engaging the shadow is a lifelong and often daily undertaking; it is a way of life. To engage the shadow is to acknowledge its presence in our psycho-spiritual makeup and to recognise that we will deal with it whenever and wherever it chooses to rise up in our thoughts or actions. The shadow is simply part of who we are. The recognition of the shadow may be the most important and radical aspect of creating a framework to sustain nonviolent living. The major faith traditions with which I am familiar offer us ideal images and qualities toward which to strive, and this is appropriate and beneficial for us and for our lives together. The problem arises when we are encouraged to look away from, or deny, this "other" within us, the opposite of our ideals. The risk here is that denial will result in the continuation of the civil war within those between parts of us who are different from, and even in conflict with, each other, and yet parts of the complex whole. The greater danger is that our denial will cause us to project out the undesirable parts of ourselves onto others. The result will manifest in some form of hatred, dismissal, degrading and demeaning of those others who are still our sisters and brothers in the human family. This is a tragic and dangerous pathway, yet a well-trodden path in human history and current events. both for individuals and for larger collections of people.

If we choose the path of nonviolence, we are challenged to engage the shadow. Here we focus first on the negative aspects of the shadow. We will reflect on the golden shadow a little later on. How do we engage the mysterious other? I can't escape Jung at this point and I come back to the assertion in his *Memories, Dreams, Reflections*, already referred to in Chapter two. It is a sentence I have never forgotten and serves well to bring me to the task of engaging my shadow experiences. Jung asserts, "Everything that irritates us about others can lead us to an understanding of ourselves." For me, this is the simple starting place, the challenge of shadow work. Whenever I am discomforted, annoyed in some way, I have entered my shadowland, and there is work to be done.

In my own reflections I have created a collection of words that are like steps in a process. This can be helpful as long as we don't turn these words into another simple fixative, or concretise them as steps into a rigid fixed order. We may well have to reorganise the various steps in specific circumstances, what matters is that we reflect with serious intent toward an inclusive attitude. To engage shadow is to: acknowledge, accept, welcome, listen, embrace, include, integrate, reconcile.

When we act out of "character," and seem baffled as to from where within such an expression arises, when we explode internally in a violent fantasy, or externally in a tsunami of unkind words, when we sneer at another, or make a snide, critical remark, the shadow energy is active. When we cut down, dismiss or demean another in our thoughts or conversations, when we act out the opposite of our own ideals, the shadow is with us. To acknowledge the presence, "I am in shadowland," can begin the process. We then accept where we are, and what we have thought, said or acted out. We do not make light of it, run from it or push it away, rather we own up; "I just said this, did that, thought this." The next step may seem odd, but it is important. We welcome this shadow aspect and recognise that we have something to learn here. "Welcome, shadow, what is it you would teach me now?" I heard a tape of a talk Richard Rohr gave in Perth, Australia, in 2006, in which he refers to such action as the welcome prayer. We first locate the discomfort in our body, and this helps us focus on the experience directly, rather than moving away from it into thinking about it. What matters here is that we connect as honestly as we can to this mysterious other. We welcome and try to listen in to our experience. What does this action, or thought, tell me about me? Who was I in that moment? What am I expressing beneath my words? What is driving me to act, or think in this way? These questions are an attempt to listen to the wisdom hidden away in the corners of the shadow. We may find that we can actually enter into dialogue with this other and ask what he or she invites us to learn.

Having made the effort to give positive value to the shadow expression by listening to the deeper meaning in this experience, we are able to embrace this shadow aspect as a part of who we are. We may find it helpful to imagine a hug, embracing the part of us who has spoken or thought the shadow attitude. There is value for us here, and we now claim it. This was the chosen action of the man mentioned earlier who encountered his rage. To choose in our imaginations to embrace the shadow other helps us to find a way to include this aspect of ourselves in our village of self-understanding. "I realise that part of me is judgemental and critical of others who don't measure up to my standards." "I realise that I have a vengeful part of me within who wants to see others suffer for their misdeeds." The learning can go deeper when we reflect on how we turn this negative opinion against ourselves as well as others, and trace its origins as best we can into our own history. These statements represent attempts to integrate these insights about our shadow into our self-understanding. Such reflection can be humbling, even humiliating, when we realise just how unfair or unkind we can be toward others, and toward ourselves. Such a time of being brought low by our reflections is often the first step of being raised up into a new and more compassionate attitude toward ourselves and toward others. I remember a line that I heard decades ago that stays with me" "The way up often begins with the way down." This is reconciling work within the soul and in relation to others.

The overall dynamic of this work is reconciliation. As mentioned earlier, it is a key characteristic of the nonviolent way of life It is to make enemies into friends. Honest inner soul work paves the way for a greater compassion for ourselves in all our complexity and then for others as well.

Shadow work involves withdrawing the projections that we have put out onto others. Again, this work is a lifelong exercise that must be undertaken whenever we experience the discomfort that alerts us to the presence of shadow and the danger of our violence in projecting the unwanted parts of ourselves onto others.

When discussing this with some, the question often arises as to what this process has to say about the others who may have triggered the shadow episode. The fact that my shadow is triggered by someone else's behaviour or words does not mean that this is simply my problem. If the other person has expressed a selfish point of view, or a self-righteous attitude, it may still be true of that person. That may or may not be a fact that I am able to address. What matters here is that I deal first with my projection onto the other, so that I can then decide whether a response is appropriate or necessary, and how I might make such a response that is nonviolent and that seeks a larger truth, or contributes to an honest and respectful disagreement.

In trying to take my own advice here, I find that a first port of call in engaging the shadow is my journal. My journal, along with the dreams, is my daily companion in the practice of self-reflection that is core to sustaining nonviolent living. Here in the journal I can describe and reflect on an experience or encounter in whatever colourful language I choose to use. Here I am able to let the shadow speak its point of view ... clearly and without restraint. The journal content is intensely personal in this instance and I usually do not share this material with anyone else. The simple writing and reflections actually begins the steps involved in engaging with the shadow. The acknowledgement, acceptance and welcome often include a question like, "What about that person's behaviour or remark reminds me of me?" "How am I like that?" "When have I seen myself doing something like that?" The attention shifts quickly from the other person now to me, and to my capacity to act or speak in ways I have witnessed "out there." I may not actually do what I have seen, or speak what I have heard, but the capacity resides within me. The journal for me is an essential tool for this reflective shadow work.

It also can be helpful to have someone with whom we can talk honestly about these shadow moments. This needs to be someone, personal friend or professional helper, who can listen without judgement and who understands the critical importance of owning up to who we are in order to forge a life that is nonviolent in character. Such people are gold for us.

Gold leads us to the golden shadow. How do we engage this aspect of ourselves? The process is often different in affect, but the process can be somewhat the same. It involves noticing what it is in other persons that we intensely admire. It may also involve noticing how moved we are by collective movements that support ideals, and that seem to work for a better life. It may be a person's decision to make a sacrifice for others, to be recklessly generous, to be boldly affectionate, to extend themselves beyond what is necessary, to speak out on behalf of people in need, to take risks, to create a work that is imaginative, bold and compelling.

Our admiration reveals to us the truth that something of what we observe in others may also be potentially true of us. The questions might be as simple as: "How am I like the person I admire?" Again, the challenge is to withdraw the projection and to consider what is revealed about us through the projection experience. While our admiration of another may be uplifting in ways, it may also be accompanied by some discomfort as we realise that to engage some hidden, positive aspects of ourselves may require us to make radical changes in the way we live. I read somewhere years ago that most of us want to see justice prevail and human dignity affirmed without having to make any changes to our lives. A person's notable action, or the activity of a group of people, may constellate the golden shadow in me. To rise to the challenge of my golden shadow, to speak up for what I believe to be just and right, to affirm the fundamental importance of the common good, to cultivate intentionally attitudes and behaviours around human dignity and solidarity, to commit to the just and equal distribution of goods and resources, to support the protection of animal species and the preservation of natural wild lands, all these may require me to make changes in how I live day to day. To engage the golden other in these ways creates radical demands on my soul and daily living.

Whether engaging negative or golden shadow projections, the important truth to affirm is that Shadow work holds the potential for us to expand our conscious self-understanding, and to strengthen our framework for nonviolent living. The challenge is to remember that in the economy of the psyche what is denied or repressed does not go away, but slips into the unconscious and waits for another opportunity to emerge. This continues that legendary inner civil war, or we continue to lose opportunities to explore and express our own creativity, wisdom and positive capacities.

If we are to strengthen our desire to live from a framework that sustains nonviolent living, we are challenged, invited, to engage in shadow work. It requires honest, sometimes rigorous, self-reflection, it may well challenge our long held and treasured ideals and goals for our lives, it may bring us down a notch or two to a more humble, less judgemental way to live with others. The acceptance of the shadow, and our engagement of this mysterious other within, is an essential pathway to transformative experiences that enables us to express a greater compassion for ourselves and for any others.

There are several benefits from shadow work that have been implied and here I want to name them clearly. The first is that we begin to develop a more honest self-understanding. Shadow work assists us in telling ourselves the truth about who we are as best we can. It cultivates our practice of emotional honesty and results in our feeling more comfortable in our own presence. As various civil war skirmishes within diminish, we are more able to be at home with ourselves. It is an extraordinary experience to come to the experience of being relaxed and at home with ourselves.

The second benefit is that we can discover the positive elements of the shadow, and we can then draw on these new qualities in our living. This includes the positive elements that we once thought negative, like anger, and includes those parts of us we have labelled the golden shadow. We enjoy an expanded sense of self. That which we have pushed away in our one-sided behaviour, will balance and expand the possibilities of our lives, allowing us to become more complete human beings. This shadow work can be a deep source of renewal and of innovation. Rarely does the energy for a new way of acting or thinking come from the established and well-defended values and insights of the ego. It is not unusual for us to be a bit disoriented by a new thought or idea, as these usually arrive from outside our present conscious points of view.

The third benefit is that we will have a decreased need for enemies on whom to project our shadows. I concluded long ago that I gain insight into a person's character and the state of the soul by the enemies she or he keeps. It certainly has been true of me. Doing shadow work results in our wasting less of our lives in hatreds that consume our energy, and liberates us to engage more easily with differences. Doing shadow work does in fact enable us to sustain the framework for nonviolent living and to engage more actively in promoting the processes of peace.

The fourth benefit from doing shadow work is that we can risk being accepting and more loving toward others who are suffering from their own shadow issues. Liberated from our old fears and judgements, we are more able to cultivate compassion for others. We may also find that we are able to encourage others in their work of engaging the shadow, and assure them they will survive the process. We may help others embrace themselves more fully and see the positive side of the work. These benefits result in a new alignment with others and may lead to the building of a stronger community framework for nonviolent living.

The final truth in doing shadow work that is important here is to acknowledge that we will not always work it out. Sometimes our shadow projections get the better of us, and then we need to set about dealing with whatever outcomes have resulted from this. We are no more perfect at doing shadow work than anything else, and perfection is not our goal! What matters is that we employ these tools to do our work as much as we are able, so as to release in us the energy to sustain our chosen way of life, the way of nonviolence.

Practice

In this part of our consideration of tools to assist us in nonviolent living, I have focussed on ascertaining our patterns and rhythms of self-care, identifying our core principles, and dealing with the shadow, as three tools to help us. In addition to these I want to reflect briefly on practices that support our chosen way of life. Much of what we now consider we have already touched on implicitly or explicitly. Here we gather together those practices that can help form a plan, a framework, or program to support building peace and nonviolent living. Sometimes I refer to this collection of practices as alignment. These are some of the practices we might undertake to help align ourselves with the sacred Other, that deep source of wisdom that we experience within us, and that also has been expressed for centuries in our faith traditions. The various faith traditions of our human family offer much guidance and many resources in this regard. My consideration here will be brief.

I am not inclined to put forward a list of practices in order of importance or priority. That feels like an attempt to get a bit too organised. I am learning slowly that spiritual practices need to be held loosely in our ever-changing lives, and the choices we make for practices will change along with our outer circumstances and events. Yet it is also true that for each of us some practices may well endure over many decades.

For me, the practice of self-reflection is essential. It is through these times of reflection that we continue to cultivate a growing and deeper awareness of who we are, of what we consider important in life, and to what we are drawn as our point of view in our shared life. Self-reflection is essential to being aware of the shadow and its ongoing presence and sometimes its eruptions into daily living. Self-reflection assists me in understanding my emotional reactions to other people and situations, and the projections I place out there on others. Self-reflection includes the discipline of questioning myself in terms of motives and feelings. It assists me in naming my fears, and those ways in which I hold myself back in life. Equally in importance, it encourages me to name and claim my dreams and hopes. It is an essential tool to support my hope for a nonviolent attitude and practices in life.

The ongoing process of self-reflection, for me, works best in my daily journal writing. I have been writing in my journals now since I was in my teens. In my younger years there were times when these written reflections were intermittent. I remember periods as long as six months when I did not write at all. I note now that it was from the mid life transition onward that my writing became more regular and then daily. I suppose this happened for a variety of reasons. One is that I realised I had a gold mine of wisdom right at hand, and I was foolish not to mine it. Another was due to my working one to one with others, and realising I could not ask of others what I did not practice. Another reason was simply to achieve some deeper understanding of the increasing complexity of my life. Journal writing is now a central practice in preparing me to be present with others in reflection, and a practice that contributes to my personal wellness. No longer do I see it as an option or luxury, but an essential practice. I now rarely miss a day, and when I do, things feel a bit off. Most days begin with my journal and a cup of tea or two (cup and saucer and leaf tea, thanks).

The journal is not only a place to record negative experiences or complex reactions to life, it is also the central forum for my creative thinking. I have planned many presentations for others in the journal, and, at times, when a bit rushed in younger years, I have delivered presentations directly from the journal notes. It is in the journal that new projects are often brought to birth, including these reflections here and sketches with notes for art works. The journal is my primary resource in sorting out all the inner activities that inform and create the energy for my daily living.

Journal writing style is a highly individual matter. I write in full sentences with a bit of personal shorthand mixed in. I note that some others do write in half sentences or thoughts, or key words. I choose to write in pencil in a book, others do so now on their various electronic devices and mobile phones. The various ways people keep a journal these days are endless, what matters is that we use some such tool to sustain and deepen our capacity to reflect on our lives. Socrates is credited with having said, "The unexamined life is not worth living." I would push it a bit further and assert that the inability to reflect on our lives, our experiences, and our reactions to others is a dangerous way to wander unconsciously through life, especially as we tend to assign to others responsibility for our own shortcomings and difficulties.

As I look back over my life I realise that I have long supported this practice of self-reflection with the practice of having someone I trust with whom to speak about my unfolding life. They are variously labelled friends, therapists, spiritual directors, companions and confessors. These are the ones with whom I can share without fear of judgement, in the hope of hearing some reflection back to me about my angers, fears, hopes and my dreams. These are they who have challenged me, questioned me, and my ideas, when I have ranted on about this or that, and who have also supported and encouraged me when something new is birthing. These are they whose counsel and advice I take on board seriously, the ones to whom I will listen. I might add that, as for most of us, these are few! These people, over the years have required of me a kind of humility and vulnerability as I have placed my life, dreams and thoughts before them. Sometimes this has taken substantial courage, and often the reward has been great. I can't now imagine trying to engage my life without the ongoing help of someone, or several people, who function as companions, and who help me navigate the unfolding pathway as best I can.

I have mentioned dreams, but do so again here in order to underscore their importance for me. I sometimes refer to dreams as "letters from home," stories that are given to me in sleep that offer me endless insight, guidance, confirmation and wisdom. The dreams are the stories from the deep unconscious and have all the hallmarks of sacred stories. Faith traditions have their sacred texts that many share together and to which they look for inspiration and insight. The dreams are individual sacred texts for each of us that offer the same. I note that, for me, shadow issues, or projections onto others, often come to my awareness first through a dream. New agendas for my consideration often emerge through the images of a new and unfamiliar person with whom I relate. The dreams are a primary way through which I engage the mystery and wisdom of the unconscious, and these stories help me be aware of what it is that I need to consider in order to support my desire to live nonviolently and to work for peace.

Self-reflection, writing in the journal, recording and working with the dreams, and sharing with a companion, are all ways that assist us in living a nonviolent life. Through these practices we can be open to the urgings of the soul to pursue creative ideas and activities that enlarge us and help us create meaning and purpose in our lives. Through these practices we can also track shadow activity in our daily living. These practices help us engage our shadow issues within so that we are able to limit the negative and toxic energy we contribute to our common life. In terms of the common life, various forms of daily news media are often full of stories and reports of incidents wherein the shadow has been unacknowledged and has erupted negatively into daily life. While engaging these news stories may be difficult, the reports remind us clearly that undertaking shadow work with discipline really does matter for the common good.

Another aspect of practice is the habit and practice of silence. Western cultures are busy worlds, yet silence is one way of catching up with ourselves and making the time to reflect, to write, to consider the inner stories, and to face up to shadow experiences. We need time to practice emotional honesty. We need time in quiet to consider the birthing of the new in us in whatever form it will take. I remember reading somewhere a story that is attributed to Jung about a man who came to him in dire straits. Jung's prescription was substantial silence for two days until they met again. The man returned with no improvement and recounted that his silence was filled with the thoughts of others. Jung made it clear that he wanted the man to spend time alone, and the man exclaimed that he couldn't think of any worse company. Jung responded bluntly saying that this is the person the man inflicted on others many hours every day.

Silence brings me home to myself, and if I can't stand the company when alone, then how can I enact a life given to non-violence? Silence offers us the challenge and the opportunity to embrace ourselves with increasing affection as we walk the inner way, and our lives continue to unfold. This is radical inclusivity. This positive self-regard is the foundation for the compassion we then are able to share with others.

Silence also can be the experience wherein we encounter the sacred Other, Spirit, or whatever term we choose to use for this mysterious reality in which we all live. This, for me, includes continuing to be aware that I am part of a larger life, connected to the life energy that animates all of life around me. In the silence I am able to become aware of that biocentric sense of myself as part of the entire creation. Silence may take me within to a deeper understanding of my connection to complex parts of myself, and of my connection to others with whom I seem to have little in common or with whom I would disagree. Silence may take me outward through my gaze to realise how I am connected to, and dependent upon, the natural world around me for my life. In silence the ongoing dialogue with life sometimes speaks more clearly. When I reflect on Spirit, self and others in silence, I am able to affirm the extraordinary mystery that is our shared life, and to acknowledge a deep desire to choose nonviolent living as a way to affirm, and to realise, what is possible to share. Often it is in silence that we understand more deeply the reality of the community into which we are born, and the reality of the common good that is essential to our ongoing well-being.

At the core of these reflections about practice is the notion of intention. Nonviolent living depends greatly on our choosing to do so by intention. It isn't about rigid rules and practices that may stir up unnecessary guilt, it is about being intentional in choosing our practices and being flexible with these in the context of our daily lives. As an example, it has been very liberating for me over the years to move beyond an outer counsel, and to take up daily devotions and move instead to an interior place of intention in regard to this practice. Presently, it is my intention to spend time with my devotional patterns each day, morning and evening. Sometimes it goes well, other times I show up for one or the other, sometimes life happens in ways that I set these practices aside for the day. The forms of these times are pretty much set in my mind, and sometimes they play out as imagined. At other times the form will change, shorten or lengthen, in response to the day. Yet at other times the practice is a bit scattered and very brief. What matters to me is that the intention remains in place. It creates a framework that I find deeply meaningful, and I continue to *intend* to enter that quiet space twice each day. If I do not, that is okay. I suppose the shift here seems like much of nothing, but for me, the shift is away from practices that are in response to some outer suggestion, counsel or requirement, to a recognition that these practices assist me in being me as I understand me, and support my desire to enact a life given to nonviolence. The intention is from within, from that deep place of self that some refer to as the true self or the inner wisdom. While I have been greatly helped over the years with counsel and advice about devotional practices from wise people and the Tradition, I realise that it is my responsibility to choose, to create, the pattern that will best enable me to live the life I desire and to which I am called. With this is the ongoing recognition that this pattern may shift and change to adapt to life as it unfolds.

In this final chapter we have covered much ground. I have considered self-care, our core principles, and shadow work. As well I have briefly given consideration to practices that support me in sustaining nonviolent living. My hope is that this consideration of these tools will assist us in creating and sustaining the framework we need for living nonviolent lives and for building processes of peace. The times are urgent.

Afterword

Well, here I am at the end of the tour. It has been challenging and useful for me. I can only hope it is for others. I hope it is grounded and accessible. I remember many years ago standing in the office of a friend in New York City. He had just received the complimentary copies of his first book and was very excited in his restrained way. He flipped through a copy and stopped to read aloud to me a brief passage. He stopped, paused and then said, "I wonder if we ever grow into our own words." I, too, now wonder. The tour covers a great deal of ground in terms of attitudes, values, principles and practices. Will I ever *do* all that I can name? And yet it sits here in front of me calling me to continue to carve out a path for life that sustains my deep desire to live nonviolently and peacefully.

In the course of this writing I have changed. I sometimes have trouble keeping up with myself. Again, years ago I made an observation in a presentation that remains with me. We are a people between visions. We know that much on which we have relied to give shape to our living no longer works and is not sustainable. Maybe we are most always people between visions, both individually and collectively. Many have observed that change may be the only experience on which we can rely. Sitting in the midst of the global coronavirus crisis in early 2020, change certainly seems to be in the air and on the minds of those with whom I talk. I hear both anxiety and excitement. I experience both anxiety and excitement. As an aside, I lament that some political leaders have used the metaphor of war to address the issue and galvanise the population into careful reactions. I find this an unfortunate image, and will stick to the idea that this is a global medical crisis with serious environmental implications.

It seems to me that we are invited now to review the world-views, the visions, the paradigms what shape our living. With this we are well advised to realise that we cannot go back, back to the way things were. As I see it, the life force, the animating Spirit for life, seems to go forward, sometimes relentlessly. We cannot forget what has happened, we can only incorporate this global medical crisis into a new understanding of our lives, individually and collectively. Out of this crisis then, how do I want to be in the world, how shall we frame our worlds, what vision will guide us? An age-old teaching from my faith tradition reminds us that people perish without a vision.

The middle ground between visions is not an empty space. It is vibrant with the chaos of the dying of the old ways and the birthing of the new ways. I feel both, the loss of ways on which I relied including faith constructs, family values, social and political attitudes and practices. Sometimes I feel very old sitting here typing on a computer keyboard. And yet there is the creative energy of new ways emerging all around. One friend observed it's like seeing little firework explosions on every horizon, new ideas and practices popping up here and there. Creative things are happening across the globe, many are moving forward with new ideas into new ways of being in the world.

I have not the expertise to outline or describe new paradigms, new worldviews. I do hold that much of what we each need begins within us, and I have taken us through a tour of much that will provide sure ground for us in shaping a lively future. The task, as I see it, is for each of us to give shape to the unique ways of our being in the world, and to contribute to our various communities new ways in which we will share life. What I have is hope, hope in the little fireworks explosions I see on the horizons, in global stories of compassion, care, imagination, innovation, thoughtful protest and bold, nonviolent action. The times are urgent, and I have hope.

Acknowledgements

I thank Brendan McKeague for the first invitation to meet and explore how we might work together, and for our ongoing companionship. I also thank our various partners, Stacie Chappell, Ann Morgan, Dale Hess and Simon Reeves, and the participants in the Nonviolent Interfaith Leadership Programs under the sponsorship of Pace e Bene Australia. Our work together was deeply satisfying and contributed greatly to my own growth and my conviction as to how I want to be in this world. The impact of our times together continues to influence me. Friends, family, and colleagues have made contributions too numerous to recount. For these over many years I am grateful and realise I am a very fortunate man. I am also grateful to Ann Wilson at Independent Ink, and her colleagues Michelle Van Dyk and Julian Mole for their focused attention to detail and their collaboration, counsel, and guidance in bringing my vision for this work to production. In the time of Covid they have persevered to produce the book and have also given me a great learning experience. It's been a pleasure.

www.ingramcontent.com/pod-product-compliance
Lightning Source LLC
Chambersburg PA
CBHW072137020426
42334CB00018B/1834